ONE W

23 JUN 20

Digital Experience Design
Ideas, Industries, Interaction

Digital Experience Design
Ideas, Industries, Interaction

Edited by Linda Leung

intellect Bristol, UK / Chicago, USA

First Published in the UK in 2008 by
Intellect Books, The Mill, Parnall Road, Fishponds, Bristol, BS16 3JG, UK

First published in the USA in 2008 by
Intellect Books, The University of Chicago Press, 1427 E. 60th Street, Chicago,
IL 60637, USA

A catalogue record for this book is available from the British Library.

Cover Design: Gabriel Solomons
Copy Editor: Rebecca Vaughan-Williams
Typesetting: Mac Style, Beverley, E. Yorkshire

ISBN (Paperback) 978-1-84150-264-9
ISBN (Hardback) 978-1-84150-209-0

Printed and bound by Gutenberg Press, Malta.

CONTENTS

ACKNOWLEDGEMENTS

This book would not have happened without the goodwill of so many people. The contributors to the book each deserve a medal for being so patient and tolerant of my persistent enquiries and requests. Although we all work in related industries in and around digital experience design, they have enlightened me with their unique and diverse points of view, and I hope they have learnt half as much from me as I have from them.

I must also thank the staff and students of the Institute for Interactive Media & Learning, University of Technology Sydney, who have given me the necessary space and time to complete the book, from its inception during my 2005 sabbatical at Cambridge University through to its completion while taking my next sabbatical in 2008; my colleagues, current and former, who have provided both a rich dialogue for the ideas that have swirled around in my head for so long as well as practical assistance with all the tasks of getting a book into print; and my students who have allowed me to experiment with those ideas in a teaching and learning context, and given me inspiring intellectual avenues to investigate.

Finally, I am so appreciative that although my family did not quite understand what I was doing, they kept letting me do it and furthermore, recognised it as important to me and to my profession. I love them for that.

1

INTRODUCTION

Linda Leung

When I was working as producer and project manager during the dot.com boom years of the late twentieth and early twenty-first centuries, 'experience design' was generally not in the vocabulary of industry practitioners. People had not heard of roles such as 'information architect', 'experience modeler' or 'user experience designer', let alone understood what such jobs entailed. In a few short years, I have witnessed a profession emerging that takes responsibility for the types of activities that were previously unnamed and unclaimed in IT projects. Parallel with this has been the awkward rise of a discourse and discipline finding its feet and which still needs to grow with support from its older cousins. Indeed, the necessity of turning to other design disciplines is acknowledged by Shedroff (2001: 2): 'Simultanously having no history (since it is a discipline only recently defined), and the longest history (since it is the culmination of many ancient disciplines), Experience Design has become newly recognized and named.'

The 'art' of experience design considers the holistic factors of a user experience that go beyond or extend the 'science' of usability (Forlizzi and Battarbee 2004: 261). Rather, it encompasses the more abstract, emotional and atmospheric elements of users' digital interactions such as attraction, seduction and engagement. It is those aspects of digital experiences that are slippery, difficult to articulate or capture, and for which there are no heuristics or formulae. This is why we need to turn to and learn from the terminologies, methodologies and models of other disciplines that are already well versed in experience design.

Scope
This is not a 'how-to' book, but rather a 'what might' book. It seeks to move discourse about digital experience design beyond just case studies and problem-solving (how to balance client and user requirements, how to display the same content across different devices, how to test designs, etc). Instead, it asks questions such as: what might digital experience design look like

from the perspective of an architect? What might feminism contribute to interface design? What might we learn from film-makers about designing user experiences? Thus, it approaches digital experience design from and through the experiences of practitioners who have trained in other industries and disciplines, but who are now working and collaborating in the area of interactive media.

This is a book of ideas about digital experience design expressed through the voices of practitioners and seen through the lenses of the disciplines in which they originally trained. The discussion is exploratory in nature and intended to spark debate rather than agreement about standards. It presents departure points for broader and alternative ways of thinking beyond extant digital design practice by mining the theoretical and conceptual richness of other industries and disciplines. In doing so, it aims to inspire more intellectually and philosophically driven approaches to digital experience design.

The ideas and arguments extend to a range of forms of digital experience design, be it computer games, DVDs, touchscreen kiosks or mobile phones. However, there is generally more reference to web design because this constitutes the majority of the work of the practitioners and it is accessible, ubiquitous and familiar. The web is also arguably the medium that most requires design innovation, having been so technically constrained in the past by bandwidth, download speeds and file sizes that even when many of these issues have now improved considerably, it is still difficult to think outside the 'page paradigm' of text and still image. Addressing this means that digital designers can no longer look at their practice as a shoemaker looks at leather. Using this metaphor as an example, we must do the equivalent of asking other professions such as fashion designers, furniture makers, automobile designers and bookbinders how they look at leather. Consulting other communities of practice allows a chair designer to apply techniques for working with leather from the making of saddles, and similarly a web designer to learn from a film-maker about the creation of user experiences.

Methodology

This book attempts to 'unpack' the diverse histories and perspectives of people working in the dot.com industries. 'Unpacking' refers to the baggage we bring with us to places, situations and relationships. In the context of this book, it is taken to mean the parcels of knowledge and ideas that are brought from one discipline into another, as most practitioners of interactive media come from diverse educational and professional backgrounds having trained in other fields prior to working in the dot.com industries.

Another term for this unpacking is 'technology transfer', defined as 'the process whereby techniques and materials developed in one creative field, industry or culture are adapted to serve in other creative fields, industries or cultures' (Pawley 1990: 140). Others have described this using fruit as a metaphor: 'Emerging art forms will often take methods and approaches that were developed by previous forms, copy them, alter them, and drop from the vine before taking the role of seeding a newer art form that follows.' (Meadows 2003: 67)

Technology transfer into digital experience design is largely implicit, even invisible, embodied in practitioners as they move from other disciplines to work in this inherently interdisciplinary field. The book makes these processes explicit upon and through closer inspection of some of these practitioners.

Each chapter is co-written with professionals involved in the study, design and development of digital experiences, having originated from disciplines as far ranging as education, economics, film, food, fashion, architecture and art. How do they unfold their learning from these fields and tailor it to the design of digital experiences? Given that such disciplines have richer traditions and longer histories in the design of experiences, how can these older approaches benefit the newer area of digital media development?

Some chapters were based on in-depth interviews with the editor. Other chapters emerged from earlier unpublished writings by the practitioners themselves. Underpinning all chapters is extensive collaboration and dialogue between editor and practitioner, whereby ideas from one industry or discipline had to be 'translated' by the practitioner and communicated to the editor in terms that were applicable to the field of digital experience design. This traversing of disciplines and industry terminology in the space of each chapter meant that it was only feasible to offer introductory concepts from a respective discipline as starting points. It is more a 'pick and mix' of theories and ideas selected for their relevance to digital experience design than the kind of comprehensive thesis seen in sole-authored books by practitioners such as Donald Norman (2004) and Nathan Shedroff (2001).

Chapter outline
The authors explore their digital experience design practices through the lenses of disciplines as diverse as education, health sciences, cinema, television, fine art, architecture and hospitality.

Linda Leung is a senior lecturer at the Institute for Interactive Media and Learning, University of Technology, Sydney and director of graduate programs in interactive multimedia. As an educator, she considers her primary users to be 'learners' or 'students': can digital experience design benefit from making this conceptual leap from users to learners, shifting the focus from the purely utilitarian motives of the user to the information needs of the potential learner? Every kind of digital experience demands some form of tacit learning on the part of its users. Therefore, she argues in Chapter 2 that basic educational principles can be implemented in the design of digital experiences both informally (such as in wayfinding) and formally (such as in e-learning).

Sara Goldstein is a usability expert in the business of fashion who has to contend with the tensions between these disciplines. Fashion manufactures systems of desire which offer consumers the promise of an image or lifestyle. This, too, is relevant to digital experience designers in terms of creating an ideal to which the user aspires, rather than just catering for the 'real' user (as is the case in interaction and experience design). Sara contends in Chapter 3 that there is much that can be borrowed from the fashion industry in relation to the selling of personal expression as a seductive experience. This can extend from clothing and accessories to the choices users make about their online representation.

Cinema has refined the ability to seduce and immerse its audiences in the filmic world, engaging them emotionally and convincing them to suspend their disbelief. What can designers for computer screens learn from techniques of the silver screen? **Carla Drago**, (a former film and television director, now interactive media producer) discusses the techniques of traditional storytelling and how they are evolving and being adapted for the interactive age in Chapter 4. **Mark Ward** contributes his knowledge as a cinematic sound designer in Chapter 8, examining the ways that sound might enhance the emotional life of digital environments in similar ways as it does to filmic worlds.

In Chapter 5, **Daisy Tam**'s doctoral research into the philosophy of the 'Slow' movement offers some refreshing ideas for the dot.com industry to consider. As designers, we are constantly told that users want convenience and will not tolerate anything otherwise. The Slow Food movement presents an interesting antidote: just as many people do not favour fast food, perhaps users are prepared to take the time to savour rich and hospitable digital experiences.

Adrienne Tan's work as a product management consultant in the interactive television (iTV) industry is examined through a feminist lense in Chapter 6. Using iTV as a case study, she asserts that the gender imbalances that were identified in analogue media industries are being repeated in the digital arena. In attempting to address audiences in ways which are inclusive rather than simplistic, a feminist perspective offers an alternative means of approaching the issue of accessibility.

Helen Kennedy researches online accessibility and cognitive disability. An interactive media educator and practitioner, she draws from models used in the health sciences, especially speech and language therapy, to understand the diverse experiences of disability in Chapter 7. Consideration of this in digital experience design means going beyond blanket application of accessibility guidelines to a focus on differences in how people learn and process information.

As a trained architect who has traversed the design of buildings, clothes and software applications, **Meaghan Waters** reflects on the differing approaches of built architecture and digital experience architecture, comparing 'hard' and 'soft' design disciplines and their utilization of 'space' in Chapter 9.

Fine art challenges its users to engage with abstract concepts that may not be easily articulated and require introspective reflection. As an experience architect, **Scott Bryant**'s art education has helped him rethink digital experiences as more than purely task-oriented, utilitarian processes which universally necessitate speed and efficiency. Having also studied information management, he discusses in Chapter 10 how he reconciles the artistic and (information) scientific elements of his disciplinary backgrounds and translates these into coherent user experiences.

The book will be of interest to both dot.com industry practitioners as well as those teaching and studying information technology, interactive media, e-learning and any other digital design-based disciplines. It does more than just unpack the ideas and frameworks from other disciplines for the field of interactive media. It tries them on, looks at them, spins them around, mix-and-matches them, wash-and-wears them, then tailors them accordingly.

References

Forlizzi, J. and Battarbee, K. (2004), 'Understanding Experience in Interactive Systems', *Proceedings of DIS 2004 Conference on Designing Interactive Systems: Processes, Practices, Methods and Techniques.* Cambridge, MA: Association for Computing Machinery.

Meadows, M. (2003), *Pause and Effect: the Art of Interactive Narrative.* Indianapolis: New Riders.

Norman, D. (2004), *Emotional Design: Why we Love (or Hate) Everyday Things.* New York: Basic Books.

Pawley, M. (1990), *Theory and Design in the Second Machine Age.* Oxford: Basil Blackwell.

Shedroff, N. (2001), *Experience Design 1.* Indianapolis: New Riders.

2

USERS AS LEARNERS: RETHINKING DIGITAL EXPERIENCES AS INHERENTLY EDUCATIONAL

Linda Leung

The field of education considers its primary users to be 'learners' or 'students': can digital experience design benefit from making this conceptual leap from users to learners, shifting the focus from the purely utilitarian motives of the user to the information and interaction needs of the potential learner? Every digital experience demands some form of tacit learning on the part of its users. Therefore, basic educational principles can be implemented in the design of digital experiences both informally (such as in wayfinding) and formally (such as in e-learning). The chapter will provide an overview of key educational theories and their applicability to the general design of digital experiences.

Whether it is notions of lifelong learning that stress the importance of facilitating learning outside of formal educational environments, or more institutionalized principles of teaching and learning which relate to the design of educational experiences, there are benefits to borrowing these and applying them to industrial processes of designing digital experiences. The rich traditions of education have so much to offer to digital design practitioners, but they have yet to be mined. Best practice emerges through a dialogue between the digital and education sectors, which entails understanding what industry requires of the education sector, as well as what industry can learn from educational approaches. This chapter examines the latter.

This dialogue can be difficult, as those connections between academic and professional practice do not always easily fit. As an educator, I see my students being challenged every day in their attempts to apply their learning processes into their digital design practices. The language, pace and culture of the industry does not necessarily translate well into the academy. But despite these differences, to be outward-looking, to go beyond one's own disciplinary boundaries to seek affiliation is important to a new area such as digital experience design, which is still in the early stages of developing its own research and knowledge bases. Kozel (1998) agrees that designers and developers of interactive media can and should learn from more established industries and disciplines such as education. Furthermore, Boud and Miller (1996: 5) suggest that the traversing of disciplines or 'the crossing of boundaries' is essential in the process of learning from experience, and subsequently, in understanding how experiences can be designed to maximize learning.

Users are learners

People who consume information technology (IT) are defined largely as users rather than consumers or audiences. This limited vocabulary for representing users of IT is telling when compared with education (which constructs its user groups as students, learners or pupils), or other media (which conceives of its users as readers, spectators, viewers, listeners or players). I argue that all digital experiences require some form of learning, even if they are not intended to be explicitly educational.

Although users of digital media products are not learners in the formal sense of the word as they are not necessarily affiliated to an educational institution, the purposes for which digital experiences are sought involve learning. Whether this is doing a Google search, looking for a map and directions on a touchscreen information-kiosk, or making new acquaintances in a chatroom, the processes of discovery that these entail require learning however superficial or even incidental they may be. It can include learning how a digital product works (such as making a call on a new or unfamiliar mobile phone), learning how to find the information one needs (such as navigating a DVD menu to select a particular scene in a film), or learning about others (such as debating an issue in a discussion forum).

Shedroff (2001: 110) does not go so far as to advocate a rethinking of users as learners, but argues that 'learnability' should be one of the qualities of a positive digital experience: web designers, for example, should strive to produce sites which allow the user to learn the purpose of and how to use the site easily and efficiently. A designer's role involves enabling users to learn from their experiences. Thus, a visitor to a website can be identified as a learner (rather than as a user), with the objectives of the website considered as learning aims. If learning is an inevitable component of digital experiences, it follows that the educational notion of experiential learning – that is, learning through experience – is relevant to the design and development of such experiences.

Experiential learning

The concept of experiential learning proposes that the majority of our learning occurs informally and outside of the classroom. We are learning each day as we go about living and through everything that we do. Learning is as commonplace as breathing, sleeping and eating. When we tackle problems in everyday life, we draw from our pool of past experiences from which we have learned to help us find solutions.

Every day, we are confronted with problems and challenges which we address by drawing on our experience and by using this experience to find ways of learning what to do in new circumstances...there is no simple demarcation between experience and learning – making sense is always a learning process... (Boud and Miller 1996: 3, 8)

This means that learning can and will occur anywhere, and is more than likely to be informal than located within a formal educational environment. Every experience is a potential learning opportunity. Therefore, all digital experiences are possible learning experiences; with experience design effectively being about designing forms of experiential learning.

Therefore, as users browse through a corporate website, they are learning about the organization and what it is attempting to say about itself. What they learn during this experience will be stored in their repository of personal experiences and will inform whether they will return. Hence the adage 'a website is only as good as the user's last visit', or ensuring a productive user experience, is critical. However, it also highlights the need to be able to resonate with the past experiences of users, to tap into and prioritize the personal. This is addressed, to some extent, in different design disciplines including that of experience design.

Shedroff (2001) argues that meaningful experiences are critical, emotional and memorable events. Indeed, his book *Experience Design 1* reflects on some his own key life-experiences. Yet there is no reference to the concept of experiential learning, or the wealth of educational research that has been done in this area: Boud and Miller (1996: 10) likewise assert that emotions have a critical role in learning, indeed, that learning is fundamentally emotional. Shedroff's premise is that creating a profound digital experience is important in helping the user transform information provided into personal knowledge. As knowledge, it is embedded in long-term memory. The user then associates the digital product with the positive impact it made, and is therefore more likely to recall and return to the experience. This process is described in terms of a spectrum in which raw data can be transformed into information, which in turn can become knowledge (Shedroff 2001: 35). It is only when data is processed or organized in a meaningful way that it becomes information. Part of the service offered by experience designers is the process of making information meaningful for the user, but it is more difficult to ensure that users will turn such information into knowledge.

Nonetheless, Shedroff never quite makes the theoretical connection between this model of data transformation and learning. The process that should ideally be facilitated in experience design is not acknowledged as an educational one in which learning occurs at varying levels of depth.

Deep vs surface learning

Here, educational theories of surface and deep learning are also relevant. These theories describe a spectrum of learning, ranging from the superficial, which includes surface or rote learning whereby the learner only retains information in their short-term memory on a per needs basis, to deep or profound learning, where the learner transforms information into knowledge retained in their long-term memory. The surface learner is concerned with information (rather than knowledge) that can be memorized as facts, skills or methods that can be deployed as required. This corresponds with Ramsden's (1992) representation of surface learning as external to the learner, perceived by the learner as 'something that just happens or is done to you': information is delivered by the teacher as part of their educational 'service'.

In terms of general online experiences, surface learning is often presumed in the name of usability. That is, the underlying assumption of usability guidelines is that users are engaging with information which can be superficially retained for 'just-in-time' knowledge. The tenets of usability conceptualize users of a system as essentially task-driven and time-poor. As Nielsen asserts, websites must have 'zero learning time or die' (2000). In other words, users should not be expected to take time to reflect on information. The criteria for usability correspond with how educators often describe surface learning. Usability principles affirm the processes of surface learning, whereby the user or learner is pragmatic and utilitarian in their approach, acquiring 'only such knowledge as is serviceable in getting him (sic) over the hurdles which he (sic) must clear for the sake of his (sic) advancement' (Popper quoted in Ramsden 1992). That is, the mere retention of information can also be regarded as learning (Vogt et al. 2001; Kozel 1998), albeit superficial.

While this is not an argument against the necessity of usability in systems, the preoccupation with ease and speed of use, particularly in web usability, raises questions about whether the universal presumption of users as surface learners is always appropriate. It establishes a precedent whereby the benefits of deep learning have less appeal as they are associated with challenge and problem-solving – attributes which usability proponents advise that systems should avoid. However, there are situations where usability need not be the primary concern, where the pressure of time is not a critical factor in the digital experience so that the opportunity for deep learning can be fully explored. Indeed, Soloway and Pryor (1996) assert that, whether a design is good or bad, users will persist, particularly if they have a goal in mind: in other words, it is the overall experience that compels users to stay or return, as users will accommodate poor usability and develop workarounds. This is further confirmed by research studies on interface design demonstrating that users prioritize affective experiences over efficient ones (Chorianopoulos 2005). Video or console games that combine strategy with play, together with complex modes of interaction that contravene many usability guidelines, are examples of experiences that have been designed for deep learning, although their educational merits are controversial. The player is not only learning how to participate in the game (through a series of button presses and joystick movement) but is also continually learning new information, actions and techniques that allow them to progress through the game. Furthermore, this has to be remembered by the player so that they can return to the game over time.

Deep learning involves the development of knowledge that is integrated into learners' personal interpretive frameworks, rather than just the acquisition of information. That is, deep learning, which is constituted by the active selecting, shaping, assembling, filtering and selection of information (Atkins 1994), occurs at the upper end of the data-information-knowledge-wisdom model. Knowledge is a product of deep learning as it is constituted by the personalization and interpretation of information (Dalgarno 2001; Ramsden 1992), and requires internal sense making and abstraction. Schank and Cleary (1995) propose that learning can only occur when our knowledge structures are amended through comparison with and reflection on our experiences. Therefore, deep learning occurs not only through experience, but reflection as well. Norman (1993) proposes two kinds of cognition: the first is experiential cognition, which allows the user to perceive and react to the world around them; the second is reflective cognition, in which the user thinks, compares and contrasts. Because this second form of cognition is slower and more laborious, it is often considered unnecessary in the design of usable systems. Indeed, it is regarded as the antithesis of good usability as it is not easy.

Perhaps this suggests that to affect users in a profound way, we should seek to inspire knowledge acquisition through deep learning (rather than just mere information retention through surface learning) in users. This means operating at the level of the experiential and reflective – no small task for either designer or user. The designer must develop an experience that persuades the user to invest time in achieving an objective. The user has to be enticed to surrender their time to a reflective experience, which in online terms, could be likened to browsing. It suggests an activity that allows the user to work at their own pace (fast or slow), to muse upon their findings before making a decision. This concurs with educational strategies for student-centredness, which include allowing learning to occur at a time, pace and location determined by the student (Evans and Fan 2002).

Student-centred learning = user-centred design?
Student-centred learning emphasizes the different ways that people learn, as well as the necessity and value of tailoring education to the expectations of learners, thus making it more accessible to a wider range of learners (Campbell 1999). That is, it acknowledges diversity in learning needs and styles. Likewise, user-centred design proposes that consideration of the end-user is paramount in the design of a system if it is to fulfill the requirements of its target audience, and offer adaptivity and flexibility to users. In other words, it too, recognizes differences in users.

The parallels between the theories and practices of user-centred design and student-centred learning are many, as seen in Soloway and Pryor's (1996) proposal for user-centred design to be renamed learning-centred design. They argue that the design aims are essentially the same in terms of reducing the user's cognitive load, as well as the time and effort spent on tasks, but with a less utilitarian approach than user-centred design by facilitating learning in the process of doing.

Nevertheless, the connections made between user-centred design and student-centred learning are still few and far between. Perhaps this is due to disciplinary divisions: user-centred design has emerged from the contemporary computer science of human-computer interaction, which is concerned, amongst other things, with issues of usability; while student-centred learning is evidently part of a longer tradition of educational research. Both have firm theoretical foundations but given the comparatively shorter history of computer science, the literature on student-centred learning has benefited from far more investigation. Within education, especially in the areas of e-learning, flexible learning, distance learning, and computer-assisted learning, the seductions of the latest technologies passed long before the 'utopian moment' (Dovey 1996: 109) of the internet. That is, the inclination to be lead by the technology, rather than be dictated by the needs of the people using it – a charge familiar to those in digital media industries – has been foiled by a strong body of research on student-centred learning which defines it as much more than just the capacity to personalize or customize the educational experience.

Personalizing the education process goes beyond allowing the learner to shape their own learning. Rather is it about *valuing* the personal experience of the learner and the contribution it can make to their own and others' learning. It is in this way that the learner is fully engaged. To ground this in digital design, forms of personalization which, for example, allow the user to change the background of a mobile phone interface might acknowledge the user as an individual with particular tastes, but does not necessarily have an impact profound enough to make the product memorable as it still operates at a superficial, surface level. However, the possibility of tailoring the entire environment in a way which suits the user and their situation of use, takes the experience to another dimension. While this may lead to more complex forms of interaction, they also have the potential to be more fulfilling. Indeed, it is the fulfilling interaction that is the basis of deep learning and knowledge acquisition, according to constructivist theories of learning.

Constructivist theories of learning

Constructivist theories of learning propose that:

- Everyone has their own representation of knowledge, or constructs knowledge in different ways.
- Learning occurs through experience and its comparison with existing knowledge, and
- Social interaction is key to learning (Dalgarno 2001).

Constructivist approaches to learning aim to involve the student in actively making meaning through interaction of some sort, mediated or otherwise. The role of the educator is to design this interactive experience. Therefore, there are a number of relationships which must be managed. Firstly, there are the social or person-to-person interactions between learners themselves, as well as between teacher and student. Secondly, where technology is deployed to mediate these interactions, there is the relationship between users and systems. It is not just the latter relationship which is relevant to interactive media practitioners.

The writings of Norman (1993) and McGovern (2002) are consistent with constructivist theories of learning in their arguments that it is human contact that will give a company competitive advantage in the marketplace. In other words, consumers are constantly learning about an organization through the ways they interact with it. Primacy should be given to using suitable technology which facilitates, mimics or compensates for, rather than avoids, social or person-to-person contact with customers. Technologically speaking, this is done through the design and application of clear cognitive or conceptual models to allow users to understand and navigate their way through a system. The means by which experience designers facilitate processes of wayfinding in a system with the aim of achieving particular tasks can be equated to the ways educators help learners navigate through information with the aim of enabling their knowledge construction.

Likewise, the management of relationships between learners is also relevant to contexts which are not explicitly educational but facilitated by technology. Where there is user-generated content, there is the capacity for social interaction and hence, for learning and construction of knowledge. Again, such experiences are designable and have the potential to have deep impact if it engages the user emotionally and personally (Kozel 1998; Metros and Hedberg 2002: 191–92). The education sector has designed such learning experiences for centuries with the most basic of technologies, such as having students write letters to 'pen pals' (students of similar age) in another country. Such opportunities to collaboratively learn about other cultures and nationalities also teach children writing skills, as well as about systems (in this case, postal) that enable such communication to take place. Yet more contemporary forms of this sort of activity, such as chatrooms or other multi-user environments, often have their educational worth questioned. Any digital experience presents learning opportunities, but those aimed at children tend to be much more explicit about this, as in Disney's Club Penguin (http://www.clubpenguin.com):

> In addition to being a great place to play and have fun, Club Penguin is a great place to learn and grow. On Club Penguin, children practise reading, develop keyboarding skills and participate in creative role playing. By accumulating and spending virtual coins earned through game play kids practice math and learn about money management. The cooperative nature of the Club Penguin environment, along with initiatives such as our secret agent and tour guide programs, also help children develop important social skills while gaining a deeper understanding of their role as members of a community. (Club Penguin Parent's Guide)

Kids assume a penguin identity, meet and befriend other penguins, as well as play, explore and travel in a virtual world in which they can personalize their own igloo. If this experience of technology can be framed as an educational one, then so too can similar digital experiences with older user-learners, such as Facebook and MySpace which encourage learning about others in an online community environment. Indeed, educators are adopting such technologies that have captured the imagination of users and are applying them in formal learning situations as educational tools. Conversely, the theories of teaching and learning discussed above assist experience designers in better understanding the processes of learning that are occurring in any kind of digital experience so they can be designed for greater impact and knowledge production.

Summary

■ There are tacit learning processes in every digital experience, such that all users can be conceived as learners.

■ Educational theories have merit in highlighting the ways in which users learn about a subject, person or process, and how appropriate digital experiences can be designed for them which facilitate this.

■ Experiential learning asserts that all experiences are learning events and opportunities, whether offline or online, formal or informal.

■ Theories of deep and surface learning suggest that learning occurs at different levels. Therefore, digital experiences need not only be relegated to the superficial retention of information. There is potential for users to be profoundly affected through a process of deep learning.

■ There are strong parallels between the notions of student-centred learning and user-centred design, and this cross-fertilisation of ideas across the technology and education sectors is necessary and important to digital experience design.

■ Constructivist theories of learning offer an insight into designing interaction between people that can be applied to the relationship between user-learners (as in user-generated content) as well as between an organization and its customers.

References and *recommended reading

Atkins, M. (1994), 'Theories of learning and multimedia applications: an overview', *Research Papers in Education*, 8: 2, pp. 251–71.

*Boud, D. and Miller, N. (eds) (1996), *Working with Experience*. London: Routledge.

Campbell, K. (1999), 'The web: Design for active learning', *Academic Technologies for Learning* [Online] Available: http://www.atl.ualberta.ca/documents/articles/activeLearning001.htm. Accessed August 6 2008.

Chorianopoulos, K. (2005), 'User interface design and evaluation in interactive TV', *HERMES Newsletter by ELTRUN*, 32, May–June [Online] Available: http://www.eltrun.aueb.gr/eltrun/publications/eltrun-working-paper-series/issue-no-32-may-june-2005/file. Accessed August 6 2008.

Dalgarno, B. (2001), 'Interpretations of constructivism and consequences for Computer Assisted Learning', *British Journal of Educational Technology*, 32: 2, pp. 183–94.

Dovey, J. (ed) (1996), *Fractal Dreams: New Media in Social Context*. London: Lawrence and Wishart.

Evans, C. and Fan, P. (2002), 'Lifelong learning through the virtual university', *Campus-Wide Information Systems*, 19: 4, pp. 127–34.

Kozel, K. (1998), 'Rethinking the end-user's experience: What filmmakers, teachers and advertisers can teach us', *Emedia Professional*. February.

McGovern, G. (2002), 'The myth of interactivity on the Internet', *New Thinking* [Online] Available: http://gerrymcgovern.com/nt/2002/nt_2002_03_18_interactivity.htm. Accessed August 6 2008.

Metros, S. and Hedberg, J. (2002), 'More than just a pretty (inter)face: The role of the graphical user interface in engaging eLearners', *Quarterly Review of Distance Education*, 3: 3, pp. 191–205.

Nielsen, J. (2000), 'End of web design' [Online] Available: http://www.useit.com/alertbox/20000723.html. Accessed August 6 2008.

*Norman, D. (1993), *Things That Make us Smart: Defending Human Attributes in the Age of the Machine*. Reading: Addison-Wesley.

*Ramsden, P. (1992), *Learning to Teach in Higher Education*. New York: Routledge, pp. 17–26.

Schank, R. and Cleary, C. (1995), *Engines for Education*. Hillsdale: Lawrence Erlbaum Associates.

Shedroff, N. (2001), *Experience Design 1*. Indianapolis: New Riders.

Soloway, E. and Pryor, A. (1996), 'The next generation in HCI', *Communications of the ACM*, 39: 4 (April).

Vogt, C., Kumrow, D. and Kazlauskas, E. (2001), 'The design elements in developing effective learning and instructional web sites', *Academic Exchange Quarterly*, 5: 4 (Winter), pp. 40–48.

3

YOU ARE WHAT YOU WEAR: THE IDEAL AND REAL CONSUMER/USER

Linda Leung and Sara Goldstein

That consumption is key to understanding the ways in which consumers identify and express themselves is now taken for granted in the field of marketing. This is especially the case in fashion design, which in turn, has created its own systems of marketing personal expression such that designers cater for particular types of consumer. For example, there is 'the Marc Jacobs woman' and 'the woman who is very Vuitton'.

In the realm of digital design, coming to know your consumer (or user) this intimately is recommended through user research and the development of user personas. In this sense, 'The Marc Jacobs woman' and 'the woman who is very Vuitton' could be described as user personas. However, there are differences: personas are intended to represent the real, to depict users as they are. Fashion articulates an ideal user, and it is this fantasy to which the consumer aspires. While this has been criticized as setting impossible standards, it is a craft which is relevant to digital experience design in that it poses an additional question to that of 'who are we designing for?' but also 'who is the client seeking to attract?' As Shedroff (2001) maintains, seduction is a critical element of experience design. The desire for haute couture in terms of the quality and wealth it connotes can have a digital equivalent through the creation of an image or lifestyle which entices prospective users. Desire for designer fashion is translated into demand for ready-to-wear: that is, despite haute couture's unaffordable price tag, the promise it makes in relation how it makes the consumer feel becomes transformed into the purchase of associated but attainable items also bearing the designer or brand's name, such as perfume or sunglasses.

As Roland Barthes argues in his book, *The Fashion System*, the ownership and display of items are seen as indicators of particular personal characteristics. This can be extended from clothing and accessories to encompass the choices that are made about online representation such as avatars in chatrooms, or blogging environments. Like fashion, these are not just indicative of what the user wants to convey about themselves, but who they wish to affiliate with and seek as their audience. Fashion blogs are examined as places where the ideal identities depicted by the fashion industry are contested by the ideal selves forged online by fashion consumers. Sara, who ran the popular Bargain Queen blog for two years and is now on The Wardrobe Channel, provides an insight into the interplay between the real and ideal users in fashion blogging, and differentiates this from the fantasy role-playing seen in games and virtual worlds.

Ideal vs real identity

This chapter looks at the web as a kind of wearable technology. Like fashion accessories, the sites one visits are intended as a signifier of one's values, attitudes, beliefs and lifestyle. You are what you surf. The company you keep online says as much about you as the kind of people with whom you associate offline, although this may articulate different aspects of your identity. Just as the clothes you wear to work differ from those worn at home, the websites you visit at work are not likely to be the same as those viewed in a domestic setting.

While much has been written about the online identities that users create for themselves (see Turkle 1996), this largely refers to digital environments such as games, chatrooms or virtual worlds that are premised upon users choosing ideal and fantastic identities. By contrast, the dot. com industry still seems preoccupied by 'real' users when designing for the web. Techniques such as contextual enquiry are aimed at studying users in their real-world (mostly work) environments and understanding web use as part of the practice of everyday life. These are preoccupied with the web as a practical item. In this sense, web designers look at the web as a form of clothing, rather than as a form of fashion. Indeed, when was the last time you thought an organizational intranet was sexy and appealing?

If practical considerations were the main determining factor in buying clothes, a very small number of options would suffice. The fashion industry depends upon choice rather than necessity. As a result, most people in the Western world have bursting wardrobes, filled with clothing purchased for reasons other than bodily protection: each generation of teenagers gravitates towards styles their parents do not wear; and many people buy the accoutrements of a new pastime with more gusto than they subsequently devote to their hobby, leading to wardrobes full of sparkling clean hiking boots and tennis shoes that are worn mostly to the mall. This chapter is not about advocating conspicuous consumption, but rather about understanding the desires that drive fashion purchases as a way of designing digital experiences that are more attractive to users. 'Fashion is balancing the interplay between the need for a person to shelter him or herself from the elements and the need for the person to look beautiful' (American Apparel founder Dov Charney cited in Berenson 2005: 68).

The tension between clothing and fashion, or the real and ideal, is skewed in web design. In contrast to computer games design, the dominance of pragmatism in web development means that it is yet to explore the role of fantasy in online identities and its role in attracting users to a particular site or product. In contrast, fashion industry practices operate upon the invisible, elusive and ephemeral (Agins 1999: 7), rather than the visible, tangible or mundane aspects of clothing (Kawamura 2004: 4). They are not concerned with actual users, or their dress sizes. If they were, then most clothing items would be made at the 'average' of size 14, the most commonly purchased dress size. Rather, fashion begins with the creation of an ideal user as a standard to which the real user aspires to fit:

> The logic of the fashion image on the page is not primarily to stimulate immediate consumption – the reader need not feel any obligation to buy, this is not a selling strategy. For example, in one issue of the *Guardian* (4 April 1997) the clothes by the designer Alberta Ferretti shown on the three page spread included a chiffon dress at £1,010, a kimono coat at £1,467 and a chiffon skirt at £601. Ferretti's clothes are extraordinarily expensive and so the point of running such a feature is to say something to the readers about Ferretti as somebody they ought to know about, and to show the work so that it evokes a certain mood or fantasy about beauty, wealth and 'lifestyle', as well as about female sexuality. (McRobbie 1998: 162–63)

This logic is used to sell much more than fashion, but this is less understood and applied on the web despite the rise of e-commerce. Thus, how might 'the logic of fashion' be applied in web development? How might online design practices be reconfigured to encompass the ideal user? How might the ideal user be a departure point for creating alluring online experiences?

There are two interrelated elements of fashion industry practices that are key to the seduction of consumers: branding and fantasy. The former is the instrument for the creation of the latter. As McRobbie notes in the example above, branding goes beyond the visual to represent a fantastic image or experience of a product.

> Great branding is about striking...aspirational chords. This is particularly true in the fashion world which deals with issues of self-expression and self-esteem. Do I look good? Does this reflect who I am? How do I want to project myself into the world?' (Catherine Sadler, fashion marketing executive for Coach, Ann Taylor Loft and Terence Conran; cited in Berenson 2005: 26)

The fantasy being promised through branding is crucial to the process of purchasing and consumption. The consumer is buying not only the item, but the symbolic value associated with the item. They knowingly partake in an act of pretence to acquire that which they want but do not have.

As mentioned previously, certain types of digital experiences already do this well. Strong branding in the games industry (Xbox, PlayStation, Nintendo) promises the user a superior gaming experience and the fantasy of being a better player. The ideal user is one who appreciates the technical sophistication of a particular platform and harnesses it to their advantage. The games themselves allow users to fulfill the fantasy of adopting an identity different to one's own in real life. Men can appropriate female identities. They present opportunities to tamper with those aspects of identity in a digital context that are otherwise verifiable and quite 'fixed' in everyday life. These include attributes like:

- name
- gender
- ethnicity
- age
- education
- place of birth
- your family
- your occupation
- place of residence
- marital status
- socio-economic status.

While these aspects of identity generally cannot be chosen in the offline world, they can be manufactured in games and other online experiences such as chatrooms and virtual worlds. However, as Nakamura's (2002) research shows, this sort of online 'identity tourism' is primarily male-dominated.

The deployment of fantasy in fashion is somewhat different on a number of levels. Firstly, it is a heavily gendered market divided according to men, women and children's fashions. Secondly, it is more concerned with enhancement of oneself rather than escaping one's real-life identity. That is, it involves aspects of identity in which choice is exercised: hopes, dreams and aspirations. For example, as obesity rates increase in the developed world, the labeling of clothes sizes has been revised accordingly so that what used to be a size 14 is now labeled a size 12; and size 16 is now a size 14 (Gray and McGregor 2005, Gebhart 2005). The fashion industry perpetuates the fantasy of not being 'average', that is size 14. Rather, the female consumer can be the desired size 12 (or less) irrespective of weight gain or bodily changes. This practice, known as 'vanity sizing', is intended to make women feel better about themselves, to allow them to imagine themselves a little taller, thinner, richer or prettier: it is not about encouraging them to become someone else. Similarly, designers ensure that their products are accessible at different levels of the market so that women from across a wide socio-economic demographic can engage in the fantasy of affording designer fashion: '...we can't put three sleeves on a shirt or four legs on a pant; we're all doing the same thing but at different levels' (Daymond John, founder of FUBU clothing cited in Berenson 2005: 42).

This is where opportunities for targeting an online female market lie. Whereas the male user is already well served by digital experiences which enable identity experimentation, the transfer of techniques from the fashion industry which apply branding and fantasy and engage a female audience on a broad scale have not been so apparent on the web. Yet creating a product that carries the cachet of one's idealized identity, and has a purpose in real life, can lead to enormous financial success. People who harbour fantasies of becoming a rock star will, in the process of waiting and working towards that day, buy albums by musicians they admire, and wear T-shirts emblazoned with their idol's name. These accessible items allow them to express their ideal identity within the context of their real lives.

Mass exclusivity: Tapping into a common desire to be 'one-off'

According to McRobbie (1998: 4), the fashion industry operates on the basic rationale that everyone is striving to be different. Fashion is premised upon the assertion of individuality. When translating this to the online realm, it becomes clear that the current practice of developing personas as a way of understanding web use is flawed.

The creation of personas is based on an aggregate of data gathered from a group of actual users. The users are then classified into 'hypothetical archetypes' (Cooper 2003), but essentially represent 'real' users and not any particular individual (Ford 2005). While this process is similar to fashion branding in presenting a generic type of person, it is more about 'the person I am' than 'the person I want to be'. In the design of web-based experiences, the archetypes are grounded by mundane practices; whereas those in fashion are less realistic and arguably impossible to be. '[Ralph] Lauren would often begin [design meetings] by describing a little vignette of his idealized customer, such as a sophisticated woman with a casual, elegant style, who loved to travel to Europe.' (Agins 1999: 95)

These kinds of ideal archetypes have been deployed to great effect in related industries such as advertising, which target the female consumer. The representation of mothers and motherhood in print and television advertising depicts an unrealistic ideal: beautiful women, perfectly groomed, well dressed, unhurried and unfazed by the demands of being a parent. Evidently, these personas have not been produced by observing sleep-deprived, harassed mothers struggling to juggle work and family.

In the online realm, there may be a place for what may be termed 'aspirational personas' which take user goals and motivations beyond task-based objectives to an ideological or philosophical level. This would mean making the user feel like they are experiencing a one-off site, designed only for them. This goes beyond user-centredness, to a kind of egocentricity. It would suggest that the website serves the same function as haute couture in that surrounding it is the belief that it is 'special, even sacred, (and has the) status of art works' (Bourdieu cited in McRobbie 1998: 12). It has the air of being unattainable (as this is what drives consumer demand) but in fact, it is readily accessible (as websites should be). Just like the ready-to-wear collections of designers, websites seeking to target women through the presentation of an ideal archetype must negotiate a fine line between being exclusive and available.

This does not necessitate overhauling web development practices. Rather, it may be as simple as providing users with ways of expressing their individuality. In fashion terms, it is akin to school students substituting non-standard items into their uniforms, such as shoes that differ from those worn by their classmates, to show that they are not identical to their classmates. In online terms, this is often seen in functionality that enables personalization and customization of software. These are merely minor variations which 'maximise' and 'enhance' the self (Agins 1999: 44, 155).

At the interface of women and the online world: Fashion blogs

Fashion blogs represent an intersection of online practices with both the ideal self and offline consumer. They are places where women convene online to engage in and discuss 'the logic of fashion' at the level of consumption. 'I love to write about where I bought something, how it was a bargain or just how gorgeous it is. I write it for myself more than anything because I love to shop, especially when I find a real bargain or discover a new shop or local designer.'[1]

At the same time, they are also platforms for the performance of an ideal self through one's online identity. They are communities of practice for negotiating the fantasies generated from the 'top down' by the fashion industry and those produced from the 'bottom up' by women with interests in fashion. Blogging gives ordinary people a chance to air their views on the ways they might present themselves to the world – as well as a chance to express their likes and dislikes in the way the mainstream media covers fashion. Fashion blogging is an emerging online phenomenon that has special relevance in discussing how identities, online and offline, are defined as fashion blogs typically cover both ideal and real aspects of both the bloggers' and their readers' identities.

Blogging is loosely defined as a practice of posting information to a website. The postings appear in reverse-chronological order: that is, you read the writer's latest thoughts first. All blogging is, to an extent, personality based: it is a medium in which a strong viewpoint, a different perspective and a willingness to 'be yourself' are essential to engage an audience. Blogs may be personal affairs, used by an individual to keep their friends informed about the goings-on in their life; or they might be topical offerings, where the blogger sticks to writing about one topic that interests them. While personal blogs are more common, topical blogs tend to be more popular, as they are relevant to an audience beyond the reader's own friends. Fashion blogs are just one type of topical blog.

Fashion bloggers use their blogs to discuss their views on matters of fashion and style, that is the outward visual expression of a person's identity. Fashion blogs are concerned with clothing and accessories from individual designers to large retailers. They offer various perspectives on fashion from both inside and outside the industry. In many cases, this perspective is markedly different to that of the mainstream fashion media. Most fashion blogs have a particular perspective on fashion and style. Some are 'aspirational': they write about expensive designer fashion that is not affordable for most people, in the same way that high fashion magazines like *Vogue*, *Elle* and *Harper's Bazaar* do. A high fashion blog may cover both runway shows, with prohibitively expensive clothing, and also the reasonably priced interpretation of the runway trends. Others are about shopping for clothing most people can afford, giving women a chance to see the season's offerings without traipsing around the shops. These often resemble shopping magazines like Lucky (United States), Happy (United Kingdom) or Shop 'Til You

Drop (Australia). The Bargain Queen (multinational), focuses on finding your own style without spending the sums required to keep up with ever-changing fashions. There are also blogs that focus on particular fashion items or niches: shoes, handbags, plus-sized or petite fashions. A shopping blog is likely to show both realistically priced items most readers can afford, but also 'aspirational' items that are admired and identified with by many readers, but affordable for very few. This gives readers a chance to become more knowledgeable about the top end choices, while simultaneously engaging in consumption relevant to their actual lives.

Fashion blogs not only exemplify the convergence of the online and offline at the level of the individual fashion blogger/follower, but also at the level of industry. They demonstrate how an online product can generate its own industry and economy on the 'coat tails' of another: 'the fashion media does indeed function as a pillar of support for the industry' (McRobbie 1998: 151). The television series *Sex and the City*, with its huge female following, offered a successful crossover between the fashion and media industries. The appeal of the four main women protagonists in the show were arguably 'ideal archetypes' despite their flaws. Female viewers affiliated with one or more the characters and aspired to the (mostly designer) clothes worn by them which were not only featured on the show but in fashion magazines. This, in turn, generated interest in the particular labels, clothing items and where these could be purchased. The increased sales in Manolo Blahnik shoes which resulted from the show can be attributed to this symbiotic relationship between the media and fashion industries.

Fashion blogs are also indicative of this industrial interdependence. However, in an online context, there is much more opportunity for consumer representation. They are important because while the clothing and apparel business is enormous and has universal impact, it has been seen as lacking truly independent voices. Fashion blogs offer women a forum to comment on the work of designers, and to speak back to designers. They are disrupting the chasm that has traditionally existed between fashion expert and victim, professional and amateur – whereby industry determined the 'ideal selves' to which women should aspire. They offer a space for the female consumer to construct her own 'ideal self' in response to those set by industry, providing a dialogue from the 'grassroots': 'I believe it is so important to have a positive self image and to take care of yourself. Key ideas are first learn to love your face without makeup, your body without clothes and your hair without chemicals.'[1]

This is more than just user-generated content, but rather a cacophony of 'user voices' where there was no room for these previously. The fashion blogger herself is able to reclaim what McRobbie (1998: 151) regards as the lowly status of fashion writing, by putting her own experience and form of expertise into the arena: 'I've always been interested with how people's clothing reflects who they are and how they use it to express themselves. I also enjoy writing about things I feel strongly about.'[1]

Indeed, this privileging of the personal through the fashion blogger writing in the first person is consistent with principles of feminist autobiography. Given that feminism is concerned with improving the status of women's representation and participation (Stanley 1990: 12–15), the communities of practice which revolve around fashion blogs are applying feminist principles in challenging extant industry structures as well as the lack of women's spaces online.

How do fashion bloggers represent their ideal selves online?

As with other online spaces, contributors to fashion blogs choose a 'screen name'. Reminiscent of the 'stage' names that performers use to re/invent themselves, this can reflect varying degrees of their real or ideal selves. While some people use a variation on their real name, others might use fashion brand names. Likewise, the choice of an image to represent their identities may range from photographs to fashion logos.

There are also a number of popular ways that pictures of participants' outfits can be posted online. These include MyStyleDiary, the Wardrobe Remix group on Flickr, MySpace photos in addition to fashion blogs. Although this brings offline identity into the online environment, there are processes of translation and editing: it is common for these photos to be headless as the user has opted to crop their face from the image.

Just as 'real' identities inform online representation, so too can online activities bolster offline activities. For those already working in the fashion industry, reading blogs and participating in online discussions improve professional knowledge. For industry 'outsiders', they are means to staying ahead of trends and inspiring the creation of a fashionable offline identity. 'I'm trying to figure out fashion as a whole and my place in it, while defining a personal style.'[1]

Case study: The Bargain Queen

The Bargain Queen is a successful fashion and style blog. The site tagline is 'live like a Queen, spend like a pauper' (in other words, a negotiation of ideal and real), and it helps readers do this by providing lots of hints, tips and inspiration on how to save money without sacrificing style.

I started The Bargain Queen in February 2006 as a hobby, because the balance between style and budgetary constraints is a topic I've always been very interested in, and I'm generally not impressed by the standard of coverage of this topic in the mainstream media.

The popularity of the site is an indication of how many other people are interested in this subject. In two years, the site grew from zero to over 50,000 readers a month, with no marketing or promotional budget, and until I decided to turn it into a business in November, I took time off whenever I needed to attend to other things. The site is now profitable and continues to grow at a rate of 30 per cent per month. For a site to grow this way with very limited resources shows that people are interested enough to not only keep coming back, but also to tell their friends about it.

The Bargain Queen is a classic example of the way real and ideal identity can intersect. Readers of the site live on limited budgets, as practically everyone does, but want to be stylish regardless. While mainstream publications often fall into a trap of implying that style must be bought at high prices from their advertisers, many people seek a more balanced approach.

I have discovered through trial and error that there are some things my readers love to hear about, and others that they are less interested in. My readers provide wonderful feedback on my writing: they shower me with praise when I write something that helps or encourages them; they call me on it if I say something they don't agree with; and they e-mail me to ask questions that sometimes turn into full-length articles.

Through this, I've learnt that the people who read The Bargain Queen come to the site for positive and realistic views on style. They love practical hints and tips they can use to improve their lives, and want to be inspired by stories of stylish people who live on budgets similar to their own. They want reassurance that they can be their ideal chic self, while also being their ideal financially secure self – that they don't need to buy every beautiful item on a magazine page to have style.

On the flip side, I learnt very quickly that there are some things my readers prefer not to hear about. I exercise a very limited form of self-censorship by writing what's on my mind that's relevant to the blog, and skipping the stuff that's not. For example, while I appreciate beautiful, expensive things, there is enough coverage of these items already. My readers come to my site for affordable things, so that's mostly what I cover. I also refuse to add to the marketing messages out there that attack people's self-esteem, more out of my own principles than anything readers have demanded. You won't find cellulite remedies or anti-aging treatments on The Bargain Queen, because I'm yet to find any evidence that people cared about cellulite before the creams to 'fix' it were invented. The only other 'no no' on my site is negativity. If I'm having a bad day, my blog is not the place to have a whinge, whine or attack other people.

The Bargain Queen is about the person I've spent years becoming: a person who has beautiful things, but doesn't run up credit card debt to buy them. It's an ideal many people aspire to, and by sharing information that helps other people achieve this ideal as well, I've built up a website with a devoted following, that is starting to generate a good income for me as well.

The take-home message: if you can help people reconcile their ideal and real selves, it can have very positive business outcomes.

Summary

- Many techniques from the fashion industry can be applied in the online realm to design experiences.
- Digital experience design can benefit from promoting an 'ideal user' similar to the ways in which fashion labels construct their archetypal consumer through the use of branding and fantasy.
- Creating aspiration requires going beyond utilitarian design to creating a semblance of a unique identity and experience so that the user feels 'special'.
- Fashion blogs exemplify online spaces which offer women the opportunity to commune and write in their own voices, as well as the potential to represent and customize their 'ideal self'.

Note

1. In an online survey of readers and writers of fashion blogs by The Bargain Queen, it was found that almost all were women, under the age of 40, university educated and from Western countries. Half of those surveyed regularly read between six to twenty fashion blogs, spending more than five hours per week doing this. Over half of those surveyed wrote their own blog with most posting up to three times per week. 42 per cent of surveyed bloggers have audiences of 500 readers or more, while one third made some form of income from their blog.

References and *recommended reading

*Agins, T. (1999), *The End of Fashion: How Marketing Changed the Clothing Business Forever*. New York: Quill.

Barthes, R. (1985), *The Fashion System*. London: Cape.

*Berenson, M. (2005), *The Business of Fashion, Beauty and Style*. Boston: Aspatore.

Cooper, A. (2003), 'The origins of personas' [Online] Available: http://www.cooper.com/journal/2003/08/the_origin_of_personas.html. Accessed August 6 2008.

Ford, S. (2005), 'Creating quality personas: Understanding the levers that drive user behaviour' [Online] Available: http://www.avenuea-razorfish.com/articles/010305_Quality_Personas.pdf. HTML version accessed August 6 2008.

Gebhart, L. (2005), 'Fashion changes affect the way we think about ourselves and society', *Copley News Service* [Online] No longer available: http://www.copleynews.com. Accessed June 26 2007.

Gray, R. and McGregor, F. (2005), 'Labels take strain as fashion is super-sized', *Scotland on Sunday* [Online] No longer available: http://scotlandonsunday.scotsman.com. Accessed March 20 2007.

*Kawamura, Y. (2004) *Fashion-ology: An Introduction to Fashion Studies*. Oxford: Berg.

*McRobbie, A. (1998), *British Fashion Design: Rag or Image Industry?* New York: Routledge.

Nakamura, L. (2002), *Cybertypes: Race, Ethnicity and Identity on the Internet*. New York: Routledge.

Shedroff, N. (2001), *Experience Design 1*. Indianapolis: New Riders.

Stanley, L. (ed.) (1990), *Feminist Praxis: Research, Theory and Epistemology in Feminist Sociology*. London: Routledge.

Turkle, S. (1996), *Life on the Screen: Identity in the Age of the Internet*. London: Weidenfeld and Nicholson.

4

WHAT'S THE STORY? HARNESSING THE POWER OF STORYTELLING IN FILM FOR EXPERIENCE DESIGN

Carla Drago, Linda Leung and Mark Ward

Stories are everywhere. They are a crucial part of how we understand the world. Regardless of the experience (a film, a form of interactive media, a phone call, a walk in the park), the sense made comes down to the story constructed. Without a story – that is something with a beginning and end, and which brings about emotional and behavioral changes in the user – conscious meaning is absent. As screenwriting lecturer Robert McKee (1997) reminds us, stories are equipment for living. Stories define experience.

Film-making in particular has refined the craft of storytelling, with many film-makers prioritizing story as the key aspect of user experience. This approach has developed as a response to what McKee calls the 'decline of story': a period where, despite the proliferation of media enabling us to connect with ever-expanding audiences, the overall quality of storytelling has eroded, foregrounding visual aspects of film-making rather than story substance. McKee argues this has resulted in a predominance of unsatisfying user experiences. Award-winning film-maker Lars Von Trier counters this by approaching the craft from a shared perspective. As a co-originator of the Dogme95 manifesto (1995), a film-making approach where story and performance are prioritized over other technical aspects of the medium (such as cinematography and production design, which are in fact considered irrelevant), Von Trier has helped create a style of production that has resulted in numerous low-budget yet compelling film experiences.

The aim of this chapter is to explore how story is deployed in film-making, and demonstrate that storytelling fundamentals, as evidenced by these examples, are relevant in all experience contexts (remembering that experience cannot exist without story). The chapter will translate this 'story-centered' approach into a digital realm, showing it can similarly become a useful tool in producing effective experience design, irrespective of whether the story is part of a fictional world. While filmic stories have been successfully transformed for digital experiences such as DVDs, CD-ROMs and computer games; the chapter argues for the relevance of story across all types of digital experiences, even everyday utilitarian ones.

Finally, the chapter will look at the potential digital contexts offer in how we conceptualize the notion of story itself. With users being interactive participants in both the consumption and creation of digital experiences, stories here have enormous scope to become structurally unique. The possibility of constantly evolving interactions, with multiple authors, and numerous, simultaneously unfolding (and not necessarily linear) narratives, means stories in a digital context may well go far in challenging the very concept of story itself. As the medium develops, and entirely new understandings of story emerge, these will no doubt influence the nature of storytelling in other media, including that of film.

What is a story?

As its most basic, a story can be regarded as means for making sense of chaos. It can be likened to the ways in which shapes and forms become recognizable on a page of dots:

> Suppose that we are looking at a random pattern of dots on a page. If asked what can be seen amongst the dots, we can imagine scanning the pattern looking for some combination of dots that allows the formation of an image of some sort. To begin with nothing may be seen other than the dots, but in due course let us suppose that an image of a face is identified. Having found the face the dots are no longer a random pattern. Instead we have the experience of seeing a face, of discerning perhaps the eyes and nose, or even an expression. The page of dots is now not what it was. The dots appear to be the same yet we see something which we did not previously see, which we can describe and identify and which was previously absent. This thing which we see is an example of a closure: the outcome of a process of closure...closure can be understood as a process which generates something from a space of possibility. (Lawson 2001: 5)

Lawson defines this process of making meaning as 'closure', suggesting a point at which the chaos becomes ordered and the sense of mystery is solved. Thus, a story and the process of storytelling can be seen as the production of meaning to a point of resolution. It can also be conceived as the transformation of data into information: 'Data are facts; information is the meaning that human beings assign to these facts. Individual elements of data, by themselves, have little meaning; it's only when these facts are in some way put together or processed that the meaning begins to become clear.' (David and McCormack cited in Wurman 1989: 38)

If the role of the storyteller is to facilitate this process of sense and meaning making, perhaps information architects can be regarded as storytellers. They organize data in ways which are informative and facilitate its metamorphosis into knowledge and even wisdom (Shedroff

2001: 35). They pave the way for making meaning by forging pathways through data (ibid.: 142), helping users to understand the 'logic' of the way information is organized, whether it is in a website, DVD, computer game or other digital media product.

That there is an end-point to this transformative process (a story) also implies beginning and middle points. Therefore, a story can be described as having a beginning, middle and end resulting in 'closure'. Structurally speaking, stories or 'tales' consist of a series of developments or 'moves' (Propp 1968: 92) which may directly follow one another or interweave episodically (ibid.: 93). Indeed, according to Propp, stories can be deconstructed into their constituent elements, but they are also more than the sum of their parts. In addition to the moves and developments, there are:

- Characters
- Conjunctive elements (that which stitches the moves within the story together)
- Motivations
- Attributive elements or accessories.

Beyond its basic building blocks, a story has other elements, particularly emotive ones, which facilitate the change process. The way that stories are read, interpreted and remembered is emotionally driven. This is similar to how Shedroff (2001: 4) understands the notion of an 'experience', that is, a process beginning with attraction, leading to engagement and ultimately concluding. Here, the story is more than a sense-making tool, but an emotional journey as well:

> An experience is more coalesced, something that could be articulated or named. This type of experience may be characterized by a number of product interactions and emotions, but is schematized with a particular character in one's memory and a sense of completion. An experience has a beginning and an end, and often inspires behavioral changes in the experiencer. (Forlizzi and Battarbee 2004: 263)

A story may be regarded as an emotionally engaging experience. But perhaps this is what characterizes a good story: it captivates viewers, holds their attention and has emotional impact.

> To be entertained is to be immersed in the ceremony of story to an intellectually and emotionally satisfying end. To the film audience, entertainment is the ritual of sitting in the dark, concentrating on a screen in order to experience the story's meaning and, with that insight, the arousal of strong, at times even painful emotions, and as the meaning deepens, to be carried to the ultimate satisfaction of those emotions. (McKee 1997: 4)

The craft of storytelling has been perfected in the medium of film, where multiple levels of emotion are in operation. Boorstin (1990) describes these as visceral, vicarious and voyeur emotions. Visceral responses are the immediate 'gut' reactions to the story. Vicarious emotions are those which control behaviour, influencing whether we continue to sit in a darkened cinema and engage with the story. Voyeur responses are reflective, rationalizing and intellectualizing the story we have just seen and heard. As in film, Norman (2004: 123) argues that these are the same types of emotional responses to any kind of experience, and they can be designed accordingly to induce particular reactions. Cinema has developed its own conventions for this. Producers, directors and designers use story as a framework for the construction of a particular reality. Story is a means of emotional design whereby the world is understood in terms of mapping emotions to events or situations.

Conversely, listeners, viewers and users are engaged in decoding the audio-visual data received by the human emotion system which eventually become perceptions that, in turn, get organized into a form of story: this is called top-down processing (Tan 1996). The user's story is rooted in personal experience: their interpretation of the story being conveyed to them gets compared with their own cognitive scripts, memories which have been labelled and laced with particular emotions – this is called bottom-up processing.

The role of storytelling in digital experience design has been more important to computer and video games (in which story accompanies and contextualizes interaction) than to web design. Meadows (2003: 18) is critical of this oversight in web design: 'Most websites understand the Internet as being little more than a globally distributed brochure. The interactive, social and narrative capabilities of the web remain unexplored...'

The necessity of story as a sense-making device remains more pressing for web experiences, particularly everyday online interactions. A story might consist of a series of messages an organization seeks to convey about itself. A compelling brand is like a good story in that it communicates the key messages of a company clearly, such as reliability and trustworthiness. Its corporate web presence needs to reinforce these messages in order not to rupture the story. A corporate website that is inaccessible and difficult to use will not correspond with the story that the company is telling about itself. The story is incongruous with the user's experience and recollection, and therefore simply unbelievable. The active creation of belief is an important storytelling technique that can be applied to designing the ways that organizations represent themselves online (Murray 1997: 10).

Studies in cognitive psychology have shown that neurological pathways are activated by story and character (Grodal 1997). The emotion system is person-oriented, and story is a means by which empathy with characters and other humans is developed. Alternatively, it could be argued that story can be a way of humanizing an organization or person. For example, charities demonstrate excellent execution of stories that elicit emotion (sympathy) and steer the potential patron towards action (donation). Similarly, an Australian bank's automatic teller machines display an image of one of their customer service officers to accompany the instructional text on each screen. The woman faces the camera as if she is saying the instructional text, making the user feel like they are being assisted at every stage of the interaction. This experience gives a human face to the organization and the machine that represents it, supporting the organization's story that it is customer-focused. It also concurs with Tan's (1996) contention that some of the most important functions of emotion is steering attention, preparing the body for action, then encoding experience into memory.

In film, genre is a strategy for grouping similar sets of emotions, with story as the machinery which generates them (Grodal 1997). In online terms, genre might be described as the 'look and feel' of a website, its visual style or format (such as 'informational', 'entertainment' and 'task-oriented'). However, the emotional design often stops there. Story is not deployed to full effect, unlike in games design which follows film in better delineating between genres (such as 'shoot-em-ups', quest or discovery, racing or educational games), thus better managing audience expectations, emotions and their ability to make sense of the product.

Film-makers understand the gratifications being sought in movie-going. In choosing a movie, viewers are attempting to regulate their emotional state. They select a movie type that will restore emotional equilibrium. Media is used as a kind of emotional 'reset' button. In an experiment in 1985, a psychologist called Zillmann (discussed in Tan 1996) induced a state of monotony into a group of research subjects. The subjects were, individually, presented with making a selection from a library of movies with varying degrees of emotional charge. These individuals tended to select programmes with high emotional excitement. A second group was manipulated into a state of stress, and these individuals tended to select programmes low in excitement. Movie-goers are literate in the genres that can achieve these emotional objectives: there is an expectation that drama, for example, would contain a movement from positive-to-negative emotional charge (McKee 1997).

It is possible that people head online to attain an emotional equilibrium as well. For example, when a customer is frustrated by the long waiting time in a company's automated phone system, finding it inconsistent with the story of the organization being open, accessible and client-centred, they may turn to the website to seek fulfillment of that story and transformation of their emotional state to one of satisfaction.

The power of storytelling lies in the 'willful suspension of disbelief', the capacity of the story to capture the audience through the situation of the characters and make the world fade away and time stop. As mentioned earlier, this also involves the active creation of belief by facilitating a transformed state of 'flow' (Csikszenmihihalyi cited in Norman 2004: 125), a detached state of consciousness which is of the moment, activity and/or sheer enjoyment.

The conditions for 'flow' to occur include:

■ Lack of distraction
■ Activity which matches or challenges skill level
■ Engagement of conscious attention and intense concentration.

In terms of digital design, story has the potential to be a particularly powerful instrument. Rather than be dismissed as irrelevant to the non-linear digital age and everyday experiences, web designers are yet to find ways for successfully inducing states of 'flow' in users. That users are often multi-tasking while using computers means that the stories told and the way they are narrated – regardless of whether they are entertainment-based, informational or task-oriented and irrespective of the particular digital medium being used – have to be especially compelling to ensure that users are not distracted by other stories or experiences. Nor should users be asked to do too much in order to engage with the story and arrive at 'closure'. In a cinema, the viewer is provided with a comfortable seat and a darkened environment, and required to do no more than sit and watch. The conditions of consumption are far more competitive in the online realm and yet, as Meadow (2003: 3) argues, there has been little recognition of the value of integrating narrative and interaction.

Traditional linear forms of storytelling

What form might stories take on the web? A simple story consisting of a several sequential moves can be seen in the 'About Us' section of a corporate website, as it has now become de rigeur to provide an organizational history as part of a company's online presence. By contrast, a story which involves overlapping or intersecting moves could be in the form of 'News' sections on company websites, where information is released periodically: these might detail the early development of a product, its imminent release and finally when it is available. These are interrelated micro-stories within the grander narrative of the organization.

Given that such online stories are generally brief and simple, how can these be made more appealing? This is not about embellishment, but the structuring and organization of narratives, both grand and micro, in ways that always offers something unexpected and new no matter what the storytelling medium or genre. It may be hilarious, heartbreaking or horrifying, but viewers/users are seduced by new experiences: 'The process of structuring and conveying elements of time, space and human experience into a series of connected events that inform, educate or entertain has become known as narrative design.' (Burke 2005: 141)

Certainly there are other elements that make for a successful story. But at its heart a good story must be original, in both its content, and its form. There is nothing new in identifying originality as a narrative imperative (the novel wasn't named novel for nothing!). However, in a context where users are well-versed in established narrative forms, and no longer persuaded by the artifice of their conventions, new storytelling strategies are needed to entice and engage users.

While the 'About Us' section of a website has now become standardized in online design, perhaps this is so conventional as to hinder its capacity to captivate the user. Such conventions have to undergo a degree of experimentation to create new experiences for audiences. Arguably, the potential of the story (even the simplest ones) in web design has not been fully realized because of the emphasis on pragmatism, task completion, conventions and standards which prioritize the fulfillment of expectations and often demonize the unexpected.

Propp's analysis of fairytales demonstrates that stories can be similar (in narrative structure, the moral of the story, cast of characters, etc), but each one can still offer something new, balancing the expected and unexpected. They are '...schemes handed down for generations as ready-made formulae capable of becoming animated with a new mood, giving rise to new formulations' (Veselovskij cited in Propp 1968: 116). In other words, it is possible to tell simple stories in new ways. To translate this to digital experience design may mean being 'story-centred' while remaining faithful to certain traditions in design and usability. In film-making, Lars Von Trier and Thomas Vinterberg pioneered the Dogme95 movement, in which 'story is king', that is more important than the technical execution of a film. A rejection of style over substance, it negates the 'slickness' of films attained with special effects and during post-production. The 'wow' factor comes from differentiating one's product through story and content, and having a profound effect on the audience, rather than delivering superficial visual candy that is quickly forgettable.

This sort of innovation also inevitably leads to complexity as new additions are made to old stories. Propp discusses the process by which simple fairytales have become more intricate with the assimilation of different genres and 'highly complicated conglomerates' of moves (Propp 1968: 100). Perhaps this is why, as McKee (1997) contends, the story has declined: it has become increasingly complex to the extent that spectacle takes precedence over sense-making. In cinema, this has resulted in a preoccupation with the technical and financial aspects of film-making (special effects, box office takings) over story. Web design has also fallen into this trap of assuming there is too much data deluge to enable sense-making tools such as stories to be useful. By contrast, we argue that story is especially pertinent where there are large amounts of data. For example, search engines allow a story to be told about an online product, as its ranking prominence provides the user with some context about the product's reach and credibility.

> The glut [of information] has begun to obscure the radical distinction between data and information, between facts and knowledge...Take the news as an example. Everyday the media seek to deliver us larger amounts of news at a faster rate. We are besieged with accounts of the world in amounts that are impossible to process. And as we scramble to keep up with the news race, we are more likely to make errors of perception... the more time we spend with reports of separate events, the less time we have to understand the 'whys and wherefores' behind them, to see the patterns and relationships between them...Instead we are lulled by a stream of surface facts, made numb, passive, and unreceptive by a surfeit of data that we lack the time and resources needed to turn into valuable information. (Wurman 1989: 37)

To return to the analogy with a page of dots, it is presumed that in the online world, the dots are so numerous and overwhelming that 'closure' is no longer possible: the bigger picture cannot be seen, only pieces of it. However, not only are traditional forms of storytelling still pertinent in the digital age (as demonstrated above), conversely, the information overload of the digital era necessitates a reconfiguration of stories as we have known them in the past.

Non-linear, customizable stories

There has been much written about the possibilities that the digital realm offers to storytelling. This has involved a rethinking of the notion of story as 'constituent elements of a system rather than a fixed linear narrative' (Burke 2005: 142). However, this debate has largely been concerned with the capacity to immerse users in fictional worlds with multiform stories that structure user participation and interaction through characters or avatars (Murray 1997: 30). Also, it has been preoccupied with the narrative consequences of reconciling traditional story media with digital media, such as 'the disparate languages of books and computers' (Meadows 2003: 4). Much of this literature celebrates the potential that lies in digital interactive technology to invent new vehicles for engagement and connection, as well as remould the conventions around narrative. These exploratory practices that surround around any new technology make possible divergence from, and experimentation with previous traditional and interactive storytelling structures and processes inherited from film and literature.

Certainly, the opportunities digital interactive media offer in creating non-linear information structures or stories have been explored more in fictional virtual realities, fantasy games and chatroom environments. Such structures allow for singular, highly customizable user-experiences that are open-ended, constantly evolving and where the users themselves may have a significant influence on the evolution of both the information and structure of the experience itself. Non-linear structures are less predictable, more adaptable and open to change, and therefore more dynamic and exciting. They can encourage participation from multiple users, offer several narrative threads simultaneously, and are non-hierarchical in emphasis. They can be entered and exited at any point, can grow and evolve and, significantly, can affect the very nature of the content they relay. They are, then, multi-faceted, complex systems that, if designed well, take on a life of their own and become, in effect, part of their own story. They provide a framework for innovation both in form and in content.

Examples of such non-linear, customizable stories include tree structures and rhizomes. Tree structures organize information in a fixed, ordered paths, leaving no choice for the user other than to follow a finite number of paths which are hierarchically constructed: that is, the story begins from a common point but may finish at any number of end-points. Tree structures represent the classic story of computer file management: I saved my document in the 'My Documents' folder on the C: drive of 'My Computer' which I access via my computer desktop.

On the other hand, rhizomes are web-like, non-linear, decentralized structures that can be entered or exited at multiple points. In botany, a rhizome is a particular kind of root, 'a horizontal, usually underground stem of a plant that often sends out roots and shoots from its nodes'. Ginger is an example of a rhizome. And importantly, just like fingerprints, no two rhizomes are ever identical. The rhizome is an:

> acentered, non-hierarchical, non-signifying system without a General and without an organizing memory or central automaton, defined solely by a circulation of states... unlike trees or their roots, the rhizome connects any point to any other point, and its traits are not necessarily linked to traits of the same nature; it brings into play very different regimes of signs, and even non-sign states. The rhizome is reducible to neither the One or the multiple. It is not the One that becomes Two or even directly three, four, five etc.

It is not a multiple derived from the one, or to which one is added (n+1). It is comprised not of units but of dimensions, or rather directions in motion. It has neither beginning nor end, but always a middle (milieu) from which it grows and which it overspills. It constitutes linear multiplicities with n dimensions having neither subject nor object, which can be laid out on a plane of consistency, and from which the one is always subtracted (n–1). When a multiplicity of this kind changes dimension, it necessarily changes in nature as well, undergoes a metamorphosis. Unlike a structure, which is defined by a set of points and positions, the rhizome is made only of lines; lines of segmentarity and stratification as its dimensions, and the line of flight or deterritorialization as the maximum dimension after which the multiplicity undergoes metamorphosis, changes in nature. These lines, or ligaments, should not be confused with lineages of the aborescent type, which are merely localizable linkages between points and positions. Unlike the tree, the rhizome is not the object of reproduction: neither external reproduction as image-tree nor internal reproduction as tree-structure. The rhizome is an antigenealogy. It is a short-term memory, or antimemory. The rhizome operates by variation, expansion, conquest, capture, offshoots. Unlike the graphic arts, drawing or photography, unlike tracings, the rhizome pertains to a map that must be produced, constructed, a map that is always detachable, connectable, reversible, modifiable, and has multiple entranceways and exits and its own lines of flight. (Deleuze and Guattari 1987: 23)

Although Deleuze and Guattari developed this theory before the advent of digital information networks, it is evident how, with their capacity to have nodes connecting to other nodes, their potential for non-hierarchical structures, their multiple entry and exit points, digital information networks and their 'open plot structures' (Meadows 2003: 66) can easily be likened to rhizomes. However, rhizomatic stories are not new.

Artists and authors have long experimented with rhizomatic forms of storytelling. The Fluxus Collective's (Spoerri et al.) *Anecdoted Topography of Chance*, published in 1962, is a non-linear adventure through associations, memories and anecdotes evoked from a group of friends by a collection of objects lying at random on a table. Described as a novel of digressions, the book is at once a game, an encyclopedia, a cabinet of wonders and a story of friendship and creativity.

Similarly, Danielewski's *House of Leaves*, is a novel that literally embodies the labyrinthine multi-dimensional journey it describes. Telling its story from many viewpoints and in many different literary styles (poetry, prose, journal, even academic criticism) the text breaks up, is inverted or pushed to extremes on certain pages as readers flick from the front, to references at the back, to divergences in the middle, to the front again. As the central character's consciousness is fragmented, so too is the readers' as it dips in and out of different contexts.

In the world of digital technology, designers have also recognized the value of products that are highly customizable and offer infinite story paths. The metaphor of the rhizome is not only suited to literary stories, but to our everyday lives and interactions. Applications like iTunes (which allow a myriad of ways to organize and access songs and play lists), or the web-based Flickr (an ever-expanding database of user photos offering infinite ways to organize, collect and link photos between users) offer numerous ways for users to create their own stories in order to make their own sense. These are narratives that might be termed 'kaleidoscopic' (Murray 1997: 155). As stories and pathways are constantly opened up, the user generates something original, in both form and content, from the space of possibility.

Examples of linear and non-linear storytelling combinations

Despite that much research has been undertaken on interactive narratives for immersive virtual reality environments and computer games, there are other types of digital experiences which span different media and are less focused on fiction and characters, than humans and everyday life. The design of elaborate means of storytelling that integrate traditional linear and rhizomatic non-linear story forms can be found in cross-media and intra-media examples.

A show like *Big Brother* deploys convergent media (magazine, TV, web, mobile, etc.) in its storytelling. Centred on the television show, it utilizes conventional drama techniques to make its realist documentary format more compelling, but this allows for only passive participation with a linear narrative structure. However, through its other media manifestations, *Big Brother* encourages participation by a range of users (viewers, contestants, producers, media commentators) in a variety of different ways that intentionally has a material impact on the show's numerous narratives. Whether it is which housemate will be nominated, which live audience member will win best costume, how the housemates will fare in their latest challenge, who the audience will evict, what opinions will be expressed by commentators, how housemate identities are constructed by the show producers, the story outcomes are never fixed or predictable. Also, in addition to the television broadcast, which is packaged in a variety of ways (live nomination/eviction, daily update, late night uncut), the show uses mobile phone and web technology to broaden the overall structure. Viewers can vote with their mobile or download live video streams from the *Big Brother* house. They can engage with the website to learn more about the contestants. They can receive updates on events in the house via SMS. In essence the show's producers create a rhizomatic framework out of a traditional linear narrative against which the many stories of *Big Brother* will play out, not knowing themselves what the outcomes will be but instead letting them unfold organically. Simultaneously, *Big Brother* is part of a larger meta-narrative about power and surveillance that emanates from a traditional linear story as told in the George Orwell novel, *1984*.

The combined possibilities for linear and non-linear stories that are based more in reality than fantasy are also evident within the singular medium of television. Jensen (2005) believes drama and fictional narrative material are more difficult to enhance through interactive television services. Instead, Jensen asserts that interactivity in television is most appropriate for non-linear content or random access content like news, weather programmes, advertisements and sports because it is better suited to being viewed by hyperlinks or selective choices. Examples include the mosaic formats that allow the user to select a particular camera angle from which to view a sports game, whereby narrative is fragmented but the user can exercise choice in the way they prefer to make sense of the content (Murray 1997: 156).

The following examples from Curran's (2003) *Convergence Design* demonstrate that so long as television content is developed from the outset with an interactive framework in mind, enhancements can give the viewer a more complex, multi-layered, non-linear experience alongside the traditional linear story.

Life 360 is a biography series produced by Public Broadcasting System (PBS) in the United States. Each episode is built around a theme, like fire fighting or the Vietnam War, and the concept of the enhanced content is to connect viewers with local events, resources and organizations in their own communities relating to the show's topic. Viewers are able to respond to polls relating to the theme (such as whether or not they've lost a loved one in Vietnam), and are also invited to send in material for the following week's show, making them active contributors to the story itself. The enhanced content in *Life 360* is intimately tied to the content of the programme and creates a seamless, multi-layered addition. But *Life 360* goes a step further in enabling users to contribute to the programme's content as well.

The Discovery Channel's *Extreme Rides* show, featuring the design, engineering, culture and industry of roller coasters, has both synchronous and non-synchronous interactive content. Viewers of the show see point-of-view footage of rides in action and are given the choice of four different camera angles, technical information about speed, height, g-force, etc., biometric information about heart-rate, scream volume, and puke factor, as well as the option of chatting to other viewers while the show is underway. Once over, the enhanced content allows viewers to build their own rollercoaster using selected segments of existing roller coasters. Their design is compiled into a Quicktime movie which can be watched and voted on by all viewers. This chance to control and participate in the experience gives the users a sense of authorship and a deeper connection to the subject matter.

Finally, an example drawn wholly from the web can be found in Carla's own work. The whatwentdown.tv website (http://www.carladrago.com/whatwentdown/prototype) is for a café in Sydney and gives users a sense of its clientele and ambience through a series of video vignettes that can be viewed in any particular order. Instead of having an 'About Us' page, the site provides a 'day in the life' experience of the café where the user feels like they are in the café itself: they can hear customers talking to one another and can read the blackboard menu behind the counter. The site tells a holistic story of the café in an interactive non-linear format.

Summary
Traditional linear forms of storytelling:

- Are still pertinent in the digital age in terms of keeping users engaged.
- Captivate with originality.
- Employ conventions but may experiment with these to create new experiences for audiences.

Non-linear, customizable stories:

- Include tree structures: fixed and ordered but allow multiple pathways.
- Include rhizomes: decentralized, non-hierarchical.
- Are not new but, through new technology, are offered fresh platforms for innovative deployment.

The integration of traditional linear and rhizomatic non-linear forms of storytelling is appropriate across a spectrum of digital experiences, regardless of device or genre. Although story-centred approaches are not as apparent in web design as in games, virtual reality and chatroom design, this chapter has demonstrated that story remains relevant to any digital experience where large amounts of data have to be navigated. Stories can be deployed across mixed realities and technologies, but there is much more potential to apply story-centred approaches to everyday online interactions, and not just digital experiences involving fictional worlds: 'Eventually all successful storytelling technologies become "transparent": we lose consciousness of the medium and see neither print nor film but only the power of the story itself.' (Murray 1997: 26)

References and *recommended reading

Boorstin, J. (1990), *The Hollywood Eye: What Makes Movies Work*. Los Angeles: Silman-James Press.

Burke, Y. (2005), 'Teaching new perspectives: Digital space and Flash interactivity', *Digital Creativity*, 16: 3.

Curran, S. (2003), *Convergence Design: Creating the User Experience for Interactive Television, Wireless and Broadband*. Gloucester: Rockport.

Danielewski, M. (2000), *House of Leaves*. Bath: Doubleday.

Deleuze, G. and Guattari, F. (1987), *A Thousand Plateaus: Capitalism and Schizophrenia*. London: Continuum Press.

Dogme95 (1995), 'The Vow Chastity' [Online] Available: http://www.dogme95.dk. Accessed 6 August 2008.

*Forlizzi, J. and Battarbee, K. (2004), 'Understanding experience in interactive systems', *Proceedings of DIS 2004 Conference on Designing Interactive Systems: Processes, Practices, Methods and Techniques*. Cambridge: Association for Computing Machinery.

*Grodal, T. (1997), *Moving Pictures: a New Theory of Film Genres, Feelings, and Cognition*. New York: Oxford University Press.

Jensen, J. (2005), 'Interactive television: New genres, new format, new content', *Proceedings of IE2005: 2nd Australasian conference on interactive entertainment*, ACM International Conference Proceeding Series, vol. 123 [Online] Available: http://portal.acm.org/citation.cfm?id=1109194. Accessed 6 August 2008.

Lawson, H. (2001), *Closure: a Story of Everything*. London: Routledge.

*McKee, R. (1997), *Story: Substance, Structure, Style, and the Principles of Screenwriting*. Chatham: Methuen.

Meadows, M. (2003), *Pause and Effect: the Art of Interactive Narrative*. Indianapolis: New Riders.

Murray, J. (1997), *Hamlet on the Holodeck: the Future of Narrative in Cyberspace*. Cambridge: The MIT Press.

*Norman, D. (2004), *Emotional Design*. New York: Basic Books.

Propp, V. (1968), *Morphology of the Folktale*. Austin: University of Texas Press.

Shedroff, N. (2001), *Experience Design 1*. Indianapolis: New Riders.

Spoerri, D., Filliou, R., Williams, E., Roth, D. and Topor, R. (1962), *An Anecdoted Topography of Chance*. London: Atlas Press.

*Tan, E. (1996), *Emotion and the Structure of Narrative Film: Film as an Emotion Machine*. Mahwah: Erlbaum.

Wurman, R. (1989), *Information Anxiety*. New York: Doubleday.

5

THE ART OF 'SLOW': TAKING TIME IN THE DIGITAL AGE

Linda Leung and Daisy Tam

The galloping pace of the dot.com industry is apparent in the 'just-in-time knowledge' generated from project-based research, the 'quick-and-dirty' techniques and corner-cutting strategies used to create online experiences. As digital designers, we are constantly told that web users want convenience and will not tolerate anything otherwise. Saving time is regarded as the ultimate objective for both designers and users.

Therefore, the production and consumption of websites can be equated to the mass production and consumption of industrialized fast food. Both are assembled quickly and sold to customers who want a 'quick bite'. The homogeneity of fast food can be likened to the uniformity of usability standards and conventions that now pervade the web.

The Slow Food movement presents an interesting antidote: just as many people do not favour fast food, perhaps users are prepared to savour rich and hospitable online experiences which have not been designed with usability as the primary consideration.

What it means to be 'slow'
Growing dissatisfaction with the fast food industry paved the way for the birth of Slow Food. As an international movement, it came as a timely response in the late 1980s and touched the right notes in people of the modern-day culture where attention to food has given way to a fast-paced mindless way of living and eating. Slow Food 'aims to protect the pleasures of the table and the homogenization of modern fast food and life' (http://www.slowfood.com) by encouraging the use of quality produce as well as working to maintain a culture of biodiversity in agriculture. Ideas of hospitality and sharing are key to members of the movement. Slow Food

is underpinned by a belief that eating and dining plays an extremely important role in society by offering an opportunity to enhance the social fabric. It suggests that a slow meal focuses on the quality of the experience and that the pleasures of the table come from a reflective sharing. Members of the Slow Food movement call themselves eco-gastronomes because they believe that self-pleasure cannot be detached from the pleasure of others. In contrast to fast food, the careful preparation so necessary for Slow Food ensures the quality of the meal and the thoughtful sharing enhances the richness of the experience. The moment of slow eating then becomes the focal point of thoughts and reflection, affiliation and association and the moment is unique to the people around the table.

This notion of taking time to reflect on what one consumes may also apply to how online experiences are perceived and produced. Perhaps it also offers a response to the staple diet of usability, which has become the mainstay of online production. As users spend ever increasing amounts of time online, the internet becomes central to our everyday lives in much the same way as food. This means that users want variety in their consumption, rather than for every experience to be the same. The sheer amount of information at hand with the internet and the amount of food choice in the age of industrial food production gives us the illusion of having variety. But the homogenous production of information and food provide a singularity which is widely available yet disappointingly superficial.

Fast vs slow interactions

In the context of food, the scientific management of fast food companies favours standardization in order to create a predictable and homogenous environment. The customers' choices are sacrificed along with consideration to the environment, the animals, the consumers and the employees. Fast food companies are only concerned about the merits of fastness, however in the wider social context the lack of sustainability in the way food is produced results in an irretrievable destruction of agricultural, social, cultural and economic landscapes.

The usability movement has developed into a science which can be likened to fast food production. In online design, this is articulated in adherence to conventions which arguably fail to acknowledge diversity. A convention is defined quantitatively as an attribute which is evident on 50–79 per cent of popular sites. Thus, it is argued that all websites should be lead by the conventions of large (and by association mainstream, corporate and e-commerce) sites: 'If 80% or more of the big sites do things in a single way, then this is the de-facto standard and you HAVE to comply.' (Nielsen 1999)

Fastness is bad therefore not because it is fast but because of its mindless discouragement of difference and diversity. It is worth considering whether the dot.com industry can tolerate the negative traits that have come to be associated with fast food giants: exploitation, homogenization, globalization.

In contrast, Slow Food is not essentially a slow process but a process that could be more accurately described as mindful or careful (Parkins and Craig 2006). As a practice it highlights the idea of hospitality and encourages people to take time to share a meal where there are opportunities for conversation and sharing. The philosophy of slow therefore is a reflective practice where attention is given to the production and the consumption of food. To be mindful of time means giving significance to the experience, to invest deliberate attention and reflection to the moment, to make the experience intense. This can be translated for online production in terms of designing experiences which make users feel like they are in a hospitable environment, where the people and/or organization behind the website are prepared to spend time attending to the user or consumer.

Indeed, McGovern (2002) suggests that interacting with other people, not just an interface, on the internet is what makes people feel like they matter. If a website does not respond to user requests, it merely represents a faceless organization which gives little priority to current or prospective customers. McGovern cites a survey of 250 retailer sites which showed that over 50 per cent either took over three days to respond to e-mail enquiries or did not respond at all. This exemplifies a lack of consideration of the customer experience and demonstrates the fastness of dot.com culture. What is supposed to be a quick and efficient way of communicating with an organization is so fast that it leaves the customer behind. The notion of slow means learning the lessons of the dot.com bust and actively preventing as well as learning from the mistakes of the past; adopting an 'act local, think global' philosophy whereby actions at a micro-level (such as how an organization deals with online customer enquiries) has ramifications at a macro-level (in terms of its effect on the reputation of the company and industry).

There is certainly evidence to indicate that users do want this micro-level or slow attention to detail in the form of personalized service, or a sense of personal connection with others. This appears to be in direct response to feeling an 'overwhelming sense of compression' (Harvey 1989: 240) brought about by the sensation of accelerated time that the future seems to be rushing at us out of control. As Klaus Schwab (executive chairman and founder of the World Economic Forum) contends, velocity itself has become the dominating characteristic of the world's quicksilver economy, in that we are moving from a world in which the big eat the small to a world in which the fast eat the slow. Civilization is revving itself into a pathologically short attention span which comes from the acceleration of technology and short-horizon perspective of market-driven economies. It is of no surprise therefore to see a certain anxiety and perhaps fear in the ever speeding up way of life (Kreitzman 1999).

This is illustrated by the swathes of people, particularly members of the older generation, who have either been left behind by or actively rejected online culture, unable to keep up and/or unwilling to be a number on a website traffic log (Greenspan 2003, O'Hara and Stevens 2006). These people who are refusing to be swept away by accelerated time cling onto a belief where the past represents security. Where the future brings the unknown, the past offers familiarity. The anxiety which accompanies the unknown future would appear to be a recent phenomenon. However, this angst can be found and traced with each advent of new technology (such as the railway in the nineteenth century, which reduced travel times by four to five fold). In the face of accelerated time, people look back nostalgically to a slower moving past. In terms of digital experiences, this might mean a desire for uncompressed, unrushed time. While there are opportunities online to linger, interactions are still primarily designed to be fast and efficient (whether this is e-commerce, instant messaging, e-mail or SMS) rather than rich, deep and slow.

Slow time

This is not to say that fastness is inherently bad, for it would be too simplistic to equate fast with bad and slow with good. Being fast does have its merits: it saves time, it is efficient and enables high turnover. But while speed is the driving force of capitalism, it is worth considering that having time, the possession of more time, is that to which people aspire.

Marks and Spencer's (M&S) Simply Food brand, for example, has done a successful job of selling their customers the illusion of having time. The 'this is not just food, this is M&S food' campaign highlights the allegedly slow production of their meals which seduces their customers into buying what are, in effect, conventional ready-made microwavable dinners. Yet this appeals to the regular customers of M&S who are predominantly middle-class working professionals in search of time, taste and sophistication. An important indicator of the true affluent class in the nineteenth century was access to leisure. Leisure, as it were, was to be free from the responsibilities of work, to engage in non-productive forms of activities for ease, relaxation and pleasure (see Veblen's *The Theory of the Leisure Class*). The cultivation of taste and manners for example, were particularly important to the leisure class because it demonstrated an abundance of spare time that was not taken up by productive work but instead, devoted to self-improvement. Leisure time is a luxury, signifying the high status of someone who is at liberty to take and indulge in the ownership of their own time. Therefore, slowness becomes a mark of refinement.

The customers of M&S in the twenty-first century cannot be defined according to Veblen's nineteenth-century notion of the leisure class. They are part of a new demographic group characterized by their abundance of disposable income but lack of time: this is the money-rich, time-poor community. Despite these differences, the idea of having time remains appealing across the centuries. Today, having time is not so much associated with notions of taste, education and culture; but rather about possessing something which is in scarce supply.

There is potential for digital experience designers to address this. The creation of timeless digital environments which attract users because the pressure of time is absent, where the flexibility and pace of time can be self-determined, has not been fully explored. Computer and video games have been traditionally time and task-oriented: arcade games are the classic example of doing as much as possible (shooting enemies, collecting points, progressing to the next level) in the limited time available. However, understanding that users are prepared to invest time in leisure, the games industry is now experimenting with exploratory genres of games where time is not of the essence (see, for example, the Harry Potter series of games for PlayStation, Xbox, etc). So conversely, the promise of a leisurely experience may entice users to take time out of their busy lives: interactive museum installations, for example, encourage the user to ponder; consumption is reflective; they inspire knowledge of the world.

Slow experiences demand much more than just time. A slow experience is not defined in quantitative terms, that is, how long we spend eating or surfing the web, but instead must be qualitatively understood. Indeed, it is about the quality rather than the amount of time, and it is this 'quality time' that is arguably missing from our everyday online interactions because they have not been designed with this in mind.

Fast production

The absence of 'quality time' in the ways that digital experiences are created for users has much to do with the conditions under which those experiences are produced. 'Time to market', or the time taken to design and develop a digital experience to the point that it is market-ready is heavily abbreviated. This speediness pervades the overall dot.com industry down to its methodologies for design and development.

For example, designing for usability generally means designing for ease of use (and by association, speed of use). The main assumption here is that web interactions are essentially utilitarian activities. That is, the internet is regarded as a tool with which the user achieves particular tasks. Usability facilitates the achievement of such tasks with ease, just as fast food makes the job of feeding oneself simple. In usability terms, 'surfing' and eating are tasks to be completed, rather than experiences which should be savoured and satisfied.

Accompanying recommendations for ease of use is the need for speed in online interactions, as proposed in Jakob Nielsen's ten usability heuristics (2005). That is, it is argued that ease of use and expediency go hand-in-hand in enabling the user to achieve their online goals as quickly and smoothly as possible.

Assuming that all users need ease and speed in most online contexts shows an ignorance of users and the diverse ways in which the web is used. This lack of consideration or mindfulness of the user is summed up by another usability expert, Steve Krug (2000) in his book title, *Don't Make Me Think!* The user is reduced to an unthinking automaton interested only in ease, speed, simplicity, utility, pragmatism and efficiency. The user is patronized and characterized by the usability expert as incapable of dealing with thought and complexity: '...pay attention to what users do, not what they say. Self-reported claims are unreliable as are user speculations about future behaviour' (Nielsen 2001).

The principles of designing for usability deem that it is not advisable to listen to users. This establishes a distant and asymmetrical relationship between digital designers and users. What might be a slow alternative to this?

Slow relationships

Hospes, the Greek root for the word 'hospitality', means not only to welcome but to equalize. In romantic languages such as French and Italian, the word *hotes* is used for both guest and host, there is no differentiation between the two. This suggests a lack of hierarchy between the concept of host and guest, both parties are equally responsible to participate, entertain and contribute to the experience.

The relationship between guest and host can also be applied to that of the digital experience designer and user. For a hospitable relationship to be established, the distance between user and designer must be minimized and there must be equal contribution to designing the experience. Participatory design methods are one way of equalizing this relationship between user and designer. Levels of participation can range from consultation to consensus (Mumford and Henshall 1983: 4–6), but underpinning these approaches is the ethical principle of respecting the user's input into design decisions and valuing their contribution to the design of the digital experience.

Likewise, this intimate relationship can apply not only to the user and designer, but also to the user and system. A hospitable experience should be friendly but not overbearing, an almost timeless space where relationships are strengthened or formed, where the moment is all there is. In order to create such a space, tools must be carefully manipulated: waiters in a restaurant should always be present to cater for a client's needs and answer questions but should not be dominating nor patronizing; likewise, a system should quietly serve a user's demands through their engagement with the interface without pressuring them to leave once their 'task' is achieved. Both a website and a dining table can act as a physical and mental refuge from a fast-paced life.

Slow Food asserts that plate and the planet are interconnected, and asks us to extend our care by paying attention to what we eat. In terms of everyday food consumption, this could be as simple as choosing where you buy your food so that it will directly benefit the farmer rather than just the distributors. Choosing to spend time on your food rather than grabbing a burger at a fast food joint means investing time and thought to the people around us, seeing ourselves as part of a community rather than individuals in isolation. Such a holistic view on production and consumption that is premised on a model that is ethical and sustainable, can also be implemented in digital contexts as part of a mindful or careful way of designing that asks us to consider the other (the client, the user) and the nature of our relationship to them.

Being slow in a fast world

There are possibilities for taking a slow approach to production, so that it is reflective and considers the consequences for others. Take the example of the television program, *Ready, Steady, Cook!* which has been running on British television since 1994. Celebrity chefs team up with contestants as their helpers and are asked to create a meal in twenty minutes with a bag of surprise ingredients in front of a studio audience. Although the planning and preparation time of the dishes is short, expert knowledge of the culinary products ensures variety and quality in what is eventually cooked. The thoughtful design, production and presentation of the dishes – as well as the close working relationship between the chef and consumer – means that it qualifies, contrary to its abbreviated timeframe, as 'slow food' rather than 'fast food'.

Similarly, in digital experience design, there is potential to be slow in a fast environment. Although digital media production is undeniably fast, it translates to being mindful of what is created for clients and their consumers. It requires a questioning of whether we have fallen into the equivalent rut of fast food production: pre-preparing ingredients, freeze-dried buns, pre-cut dehydrated vegetables fitted into a polystyrene box and placed in a paper bag. Is this the best that can be offered to clients, who would like to think that their online presence demands attention, that consumers would take time to discover or use their unique product or service? More importantly, is it a sustainable (rather than a disposable) model of production and consumption?

The valuing of slowness in digital media production can be seen in the investment of time, despite its scarcity and luxury, by designers in getting to know clients and their customers well, and giving attention to detail in promoting the client's products in the digital environment. As mentioned previously, slowness can be demonstrated by an ethic of care and hospitality that a client experiences working with a designer. The client must educate the designer in the products or services that they offer, while the designer must educate the client in ways of creating a digital experience that will best facilitate users' exposure to these products or services. Both client and designer collaborate to design the experience for the end user.

As in *Ready, Steady, Cook!*, the contestant (or client) supplies the ingredients, and in discussion with the chef (designer), determines how these should be prepared, cooked and presented to inspire the viewer (user) to make it themselves at home. This attempt to generate an intimate familiarity with a product or activity before intended engagement can also be seen in cookbooks, where dishes are photographed in close-up and the reader is invited to experience the food visually before making it (Norman 2004: 102 – see his discussion of the Japanese lunchbox). These examples also demonstrate the potential of being slow (through acknowledging the work and beauty that lies behind a dish) in fast environments (where a recipe promises that the dish can be produced in a certain amount of time).

Current practice in online design seems to conflate the necessity of speed in production with that in consumption. Yet it is possible to have fast production for slow consumption in the digital arena. Consumers can be enticed to invest quality time and reflection to the client's product or service. As Norman (2004: 94) observes, this illustrates usability principles in reverse: it is about making something desirable through its lack of availability. The promise of a product is so high that it demands time from those who want to experience it. Although time is valuable, they are prepared to sacrifice it. The role of the digital designer is to ensure that this experience is not a mere pitstop in a user's web surfing, a glance between multi-tasking, listening to the radio and/or watching the news. The association of slowness with leisure, timelessness and luxury is seductive in its allure of 'stealing time' out of the user's day for non-productive but reflective work. Again, it is about the possibility of being slow in a fast world.

> we need to recognize that speed itself is not a universal good. Not only has the time of construction shrunk, so too has the time allowed for research, design, development and

documentation...Lack of time for reflection is, ironically, the greatest barrier for critical thinking about the future. Speed does not lead to innovation, rather in the process of design it forces reliance on conventions and the eschewing of alternatives. (Kaji-O'Grady 2006: 11)

Summary

- The approaches and processes of the digital media industry can be equated to the fast food industry in terms of the pace of production and emphasis on speed, ease and convenience.
- The 'slow' movement offers the dot.com industry lessons in the value of mindful production which does not homogenize or patronize the user experience.
- Slowness offers dot.com clients the attraction of being considered thoughtfully and uniquely by their customers.
- Being slow in a fast world can appeal to consumers through its promise of timelessness, leisure and status.
- Slow values in digital experience design can be translated as an ability to operate with integrity and sustainability in a fast world, which includes a willingness to invest time in clients and their customers.

References and *recommended reading

Greenspan, R. (2003), 'Internet not for everyone' [Online] Available: http://www.clickz.com/stats/ big_picture/demographics/article.php/2192251. Accessed April 16 2008.

Harvey, D. (1989), The Condition of Postmodernity: An Enquiry into the Origins of Cultural Change. Oxford: Blackwell.

Kaji-O'Grady, S. (2006), 'Future fast', U: magazine. Sydney: University of Technology Sydney. April.

Kreitzman, L. (1999), 24-hour Society. London: Profile Books.

Krug, S. (2000), Don't Make Me Think! Indianapolis: New Riders.

McGovern, G. (2002), 'The myth of interactivity on the Internet', New Thinking [Online] Available: http:// gerrymcgovern.com/nt/2002/nt_2002_03_18_interactivity.htm. Accessed August 6 2008.

Mumford, E. and Henshall, D. (1983), Designing Participatively: a Participative Approach to Computer Systems Design. Manchester: Manchester Business School.

Nielsen, J. (1999), 'When bad design becomes the standard' [Online] Available: http://www.useit.com/ alertbox/991114.html. Accessed August 6 2008.

Nielsen, J. (2001), 'First rule of usability? Don't listen to users' [Online] Available: http://www.useit.com/ alertbox/20010805.html. Accessed August 6 2008.

Nielsen, J. (2005), 'Ten usability heuristics' [Online] Available: http://www.useit.com/papers/heuristic/ heuristic_list.html. Accessed August 6 2008.

Norman, D. (2004), Emotional Design: Why we Love (or Hate) Everyday Things. New York: Basic Books.

O'Hara, K. and Stevens, D. (2006), Inequality.com: Power, Poverty and the Digital Divide. Oxford: Oneworld.

*Parkins, W. and Craig, G. (2006), Slow Living. Oxford: Berg.

Veblen, T. (1967), The Theory of the Leisure Class. London: Penguin.

6

THE PERSONAL IS THE POLITICAL: WHY FEMINISM IS IMPORTANT TO EXPERIENCE DESIGN

Linda Leung and Adrienne Tan

In their many responses to the media industries, feminism has asked that media producers understand the complexity and diversity of their audiences so that they are addressed in ways which are inclusive rather than simplistic.

While analogue media has improved its capacity to cater for women, the digital world still has lessons to learn and apply in terms designing with consideration to the emotional and personal experiences of women. In particular, interactive television (iTV) offers an illustration of the new forms of gendered digital media production and representation. These are currently male-oriented and lack appeal to women. The particular questions to be addressed in this chapter are:

- What role does gender difference play in understanding audiences?
- Using iTV as a case study, how is gender difference designed and manifest?
- How might personalization speak to diversity while offering inclusiveness? What are some examples?
- How might personalization be regarded as feminist?

The role of gender
The role of gender has been widely researched in studies of media production, representation and consumption. These areas have been found to be interconnected such that if producers are not representative of the demographic, political and cultural range that can be found in society,

then the content they produce also tends to be narrowly constituted. This applies as much to traditional/analogue/broadcast media as it does to digital/interactive media. The role of the television producer, for example, has been described as similar to 'the governor of a small colony' (Tunstall 1993: 4). This is telling in its allusion to the primarily male and white profile of television production. Likewise, such allegations have also been made in relation to newspaper ownership, film and radio production (Leung 2005: 31–33). In turn, this has informed the large amount of work that has been done examining gendered media representations, that is, the ways in which men and women are depicted stereotypically in the media (Jackson 1993; Williamson 1978; Kaplan 1983; Baehr and Dyer 1987). These studies have found that on television, men largely adopt traditional roles as such as 'breadwinner', 'hero' or 'villain' whilst women mostly play parts that characterize their 'expected' position in society of either 'mother', 'wife' or 'vixen'. Such research has subsequently led to recommendations and calls for action in ensuring that the staff and structures of media organizations reflect the broader community, and informed the changing media landscape that has produced a wider range of contemporary depictions of women.

In the relatively short history of the internet, it has similarly been found that the dominant group to set norms in the online world are male and white (Kendall 1999: 59, 66). Back in 1993, it was claimed that as much as 95 per cent of computer networks were male. Even in the twenty-first century, when internet use has become more pervasive and gender-balanced in mainly Western countries, studies have found online representations of women to be predominantly sexualized (Nakamura 2002) and do not speak to female internet users (Leung 2005). Pornography remains as one of the primary activities of the internet. Norman (2004: 43) notes that the design of video games by 'young excitable males' for 'young excitable males' has restricted its potential to appeal to young, excitable females. Even with the advent of social networking, there are sites such as Videosift (http://www.videosift.com) which are as much as 84 per cent male.

Why does this matter? It is important because it is not only about inclusiveness for the sake of equity, but about markets that are not being served well by the media industries. Furthermore, it is relevant to everyone – men and women – working in any kind of media production as it is concerned with issues of access, accessibility and audiences. In short, it has as much a legal and business objective as one of equality.

What has feminism got to do with it?

Feminism is concerned with investigating and addressing 'the condition of women in a sexist society' (Stanley 1990: 12–15). That is, it is focused on the experiences of and issues affecting women and actively attempts to find solutions to situations of inequality where women are excluded or disadvantaged.

Therefore, feminist responses to the acknowledged lack of women in the IT industry have included the development of projects specifically aimed at providing girls of school age with technical competence and confidence, as well as encouraging them into technology-related education and occupations (Leung 2005: 68–69). Likewise, the film industry has established funding programmes with the purpose of training more women as producers, directors, screenwriters, cinematographers and editors (Caine et al. 1998: 113). Women's lobby groups have succeeded in making the advertising industry accountable for its representations of women through public forums, regulatory codes and anti-sexism laws (Mann 1989).

Thus, feminist analyses of media industries and representations have resulted in firstly, organizational recognition of gender imbalance at the level of production and management; and secondly, the implementation of equal opportunity and affirmative action policies to rectify this. In time, this has cultivated media content which can be described as feminist in orientation in dealing with issues that affect women, contest traditional portrayals of women, and offer positive depictions and role models.

However, initiatives which tackle gender inequality require just that: initiative – on the part of both individuals and organizations. They need a change in perception on the part of organizations whereby they accept the need to reflect and understand the audiences whom they serve, and that a mismatch between producers and consumers is ultimately detrimental to both parties. The change in the mass media's masculine culture has ultimately been profitable for the media industries (Hartley cited in Caine et al. 1998: 220). The exclusion of women, or indeed any major market segment, at the level of production will translate to their absence at the level of consumption, making no business sense. To ignore those markets means that it will eventually cost the organization to grow them later: any kind of imbalance necessitates significant investment to restore equitable conditions.

The consequences of a non-inclusive outlook are illustrated in a case brought before the Australian Government's Human Rights & Equal Opportunity Commission (HREOC 2000) against the Sydney Organizing Committee for the Olympic Games (SOCOG). The committee was responsible for coordinating all media coverage before, during and after the Olympic Games held in Sydney in 2000. This included developing a website through which tickets could be bought online and which provided information about events which were not covered by traditional broadcast media. Therefore, the site's purpose was to serve the wider global and local public consisting of people who could not travel to Sydney to attend events as well as those who could. The complaint lodged by Bruce Maguire, who is blind, against SOCOG alleged that the website was inaccessible to people with impaired vision. It was found that the site did not comply with W3C guidelines, did not have any ALT tags on images, and that a blind user would require the assistance of a sighted person to use it. SOCOG and the company contracted to design the site, IBM, claimed that to address these issues, the organizations 'would have to retrain many of its staff and redraw its entire development methodology', develop a new or separate site altogether at a cost of AUS$2.2 million. SOCOG ignored the ruling that they must take reasonable steps to make their site more accessible and was subsequently fined AUS$20,000.

An ethic of inclusiveness is a matter of acknowledging diversity and plurality of users.

How does this relate to experience design?

Gender is an important consideration when understanding any kind of media audience. Traditional media industries have clearly defined its audiences according to gender and genres. Advertisers claim to comprehensively research and understand their target audiences more than any other form of communication (Mann 1989: 51). Particular genres of television program such as soap opera are heavily gendered in that their audiences are largely female. Similarly, in film, romantic comedy has been identified as a genre which primarily appeals to women. In literature, women's autobiographies, 'a written or verbal personal interpretation of one's life' (Humm 1989: 16) and romance novels (Radway 1984) are popular with female readers. Women's magazines have spawned a range of sub-genres which specifically delineate between and target teenage girls to homemakers to fashion-conscious young professionals. Even in the universe of games, those that have a significant female market (such as The Sims, and SongStar) are distinguishable from those that are not. The rise of 'casual' gaming has been fuelled by women. Casual games are those which can be described as small-scale, simple, self-contained, retro, require minimal commitment or investment and include puzzles, card games and classics like Pacman. According to casual game distributors such as Microsoft, AOL and Yahoo, most participants are female (Hyman 2004). Across this media landscape, what is common to media experiences that have been designed for women?

Firstly, it should be noted that such experiences have often emerged in response to the exclusion of women in other genres of the media. In the history of television and in comparison with genres such as news and sports, it was soap opera that pioneered shows in which women had the starring role. Likewise, while women's magazines now form a large part of the print media market, most other forms such as computer, sports and business magazines and newspapers have been criticized as male-oriented. Feminist film theorists maintain that even in genres aimed at women, such as romantic comedy, film perpetuates a 'male gaze' (Mulvey 1989) by which women are depicted from a male point of view primarily because it is mostly men behind the movie camera.

Media and genres that have successfully developed female markets foreground and acknowledge the experiences of women. Moreover, personal experience is privileged, and not derided as purely subjective or individual. Rather, personal experiences are regarded as ways of connecting to others. The sharing of experiences is seen as a means for speaking to a group or community. It is in this sense that, as the feminist slogan goes, 'the personal is the political'. That is, personal experience provides an insight into social networks and contexts.

As subjectivity and personal experience are given priority, the need for objectivity has less relevance. Indeed, objectivity is deemed impossible because our perspectives are always personally and emotionally informed. Emotions 'are privileged [in feminism] as powerful sources of knowledge, as forms of cognition, appraisal, judgement or choice, and as tools for grasping the world and changing it' (Humm 1989: 77). The important role of emotions is not only acknowledged by feminists, but also by psychologists: 'Emotions are inseparable from and a necessary part of cognition. Everything we do, everything we think is tinged with emotion, much of it subconscious. In turn, our emotions change the way we think...' (Norman 2004: 7).

It is the affective or emotional system which is triggered first to give a quick subconscious judgment or first impression of an experience before the cognitive system is activated to interpret or make sense of the situation (ibid. 11).

This is applied in televison in soap operas which depict the emotional terrain of life through its (mostly) female characters (Glaessner 1990: 119). The personal experiences of the characters speaks to those of the community of women who form the show's audience: 'television soap operas...are a way of understanding and coping with problems shared by other women' (Nightingale 1990: 36). The characters' experiences form an emotional narrative through which their lives are told and interpreted. Furthermore, the content of soap operas and other female genres as discussed above tend to make sense of the world through the personal and emotional dimensions of family, work and home life, and relationships with men. In relation to online experiences, these issues also resonate in women's blogs, which as a form of personal journal keeping made public, can be likened to autobiography. Such blogs are consistent with the use of diaries in feminist research to record the researcher's feelings and ideas (Humm 1989: 63).

Unlike the other kinds of media mentioned previously, blogs allow direct interaction between the blogger/writer and her readers/audience. A blog gives readers an opportunity to publicly respond to the blogger/writer as well as to each other, enabling a right of reply in one's own voice which is limited or absent altogether in women's magazines, books or soap operas. It is not only these one-to-one relationships which can appeal to a female market. Blogs can speak to, as well as speak from the personal experiences of the readers. It takes the role of personal experience to another dimension, as it facilitates more than one person's story. This sort of personalization has a lot of potential to appeal to female markets which have not yet been fully realized in digital interactive media.

There is an increasing movement towards personalization in new technologies. The ability to change the 'skin' of a website, to individualize your mobile phone ringtone, to choose the desktop background and screensaver of a computer, to tailor the playlist on your iPod, are all examples of this. However, these types of personalization are cosmetic and/or functional, and do not necessarily enlist the personal and emotional experiences of the user. They exemplify customization (choosing from a fixed set of alternatives) rather than the generation of personal meaning or emotional attachment (Norman 2004: 220, 222).

For this reason, there are still many types of technological experiences which do not appeal to female audiences and users. Feminists acknowledge the importance of emotion in 'diverting attention away from instrumental goal-centred issues' (Mumby and Putnam 1992). Emotional design and, therefore, designing for women must go beyond mere utilitarian requirements, to appeal to wants and desires (Norman 2004: 42). 'I have long argued that machines should indeed both have and display emotions...' (ibid. 179).

Norman suggests that positive affect can be produced by attributes such as: warmth, light, sweet tastes and smells, soothing sounds, caress, smiles, rhythms, 'attractive' people, symmetry, and round smooth objects (ibid. 29). Separately, it has been argued that 'a feminine cognitive style would be artistic, sensitive, integrated, deep, intersubjective, empathic, associative, affective, open, personalised, aesthetic and receptive' (Humm 1989: 85). Thus, from both design and feminist perspectives, experiences which are inclusive of and appeal to women should display emotional intelligence as articulated in the abovementioned qualities.

Case study: Interactive television

Throughout its analogue history, television has refined the craft of emotional design in its production of programmes specifically targeted at female audiences. However, the advent of the digital era has left women largely excluded from the possibilities offered by interactive television. Subscription (or pay) TV does offer a wider menu of channels for women through niche programming, but without the innovation in interaction that can be seen in male-oriented content. It mirrors the gender disparities that have been identified in relation to the design, development and participation in other technologies, both old (such as broadcast television) and current (such as video games) (Caine et al. 1998: 65). Just as e-commerce on the internet was pioneered through pornography with men as the assumed users, iTV applications seem to perceive men as the remote-control operators.

Interactive television refers to digital television services which include interactive applications such as:

- *electronic program guide (EPG)*, in which viewers, via their remote control are able to view upcoming programming schedules and set programme reminders for each channel.
- *interactive radio*, whereby users can choose a song from a range of music genres via their television set using their remote control.
- *casual games* which users can play using their remote control.
- *box office*, in which viewers can browse through pay-per-view movie information, before purchasing either by phone, internet or through their set top box with the remote control.
- *personalized television news* which allows users to tailor current affairs programmes according to their interests.
- *access to e-mail and internet* via the television (Eronen 2002: 73).

Over and above these applications, viewers also have access to a number of programme enhancements. Programme enhancements are interactive by nature as viewers can select suitable video or text-based content to obtain more information about the programme. Programme enhancements are available for use when a programme is being broadcast. These include:

- *weather enhancement*, in which users can personalize the weather application to deliver weather information for a specific postcode.
- *sports active*, in which viewers can select different camera angles and views of a football, tennis, cricket, basketball or other sports game. Game statistics are also available for consumption.
- *news active*, in which viewers can select a news topic from an eight screen mosaic to obtain 'on demand' information.

The inclusion of interactive services and features are designed with the premise of complementing programmes. As television is almost universally watched – being more pervasive than the use of computers and mobile phones (Gawlinski 2003: 214) – it follows that interactive services should be implemented evenly with consideration to genre of show and the audience watching it. Gender-specific interactive services are evident, but are predominantly male-oriented: most programme enhancements and interactive features are concentrated in the genre of sport (BBC 2005: 18): 'Sports programming is an area which is the preserve of men. Not only is it dominated by masculine sports and male commentators, it occupies a privileged position in the schedules.' (Dyer 1987: 8)

More recently, according to a Roy Morgan poll (2006), 73 per cent of men compared with 27 per cent of women were 'very' interested in watching sport on pay TV. Nonetheless, this percentage becomes more gender-balanced for those who are 'quite' or 'somewhat' interested in pay TV sport.

Research examining the processes by which television broadcast companies develop new concepts for programmes with interactive features shows that gender is a key factor in how audiences are profiled. As with any new technology, iTV consumers are categorized into four main groups:

- early adopters
- early majority
- late majority
- mass market (Gawlinski 2003: 229).

It is noteworthy that female markets are part of all these groups. However, early adopters are generally personified as male, as in the term 'Gadget Guy': 'The traditional early adopter market can be loosely characterised as 60–80 per cent male, mostly aged 25–34.' (Gawlinski 2003: 231)

Nonetheless, early adopters also include Generation 'i' or 'Y' – that is, socially active teenagers – of whom teenage girls make up a large proportion. Within the early majority group are 'Daytime Dabblers' who are characterized as almost entirely female, active players of iTV games who use iTV differently to their spouses (ibid. 232). Indeed, iTV games could also be described as casual games and thus have a similar appeal to women of being intuitive, discrete and requiring minimal learning time. Adult female viewers are perceived as interested in 'domestic reality-based programmes, and criminal investigation shows' while their male counterparts watched 'sports and entertainment' (Eronen 2002: 76). Yet Lu (2005: 74) argues that there has been minimal development of drama for iTV despite that this genre commands loyal followings. Television producers suggested that news and current affairs could be separated into a 'Women's corner' and 'Men's corner' and accessed accordingly. However, it was also proposed that older female viewers should not be compelled to use the interactive features: 'We cannot force the features of interactive television on these people, we rather tell them what to do if they have an interest to participate in the TV show.' (Eronen 2002: 77)

Women (rather than men) of a mature age are seen as needing instruction when it comes to using iTV, contrary to the BBC's findings that its use is not gender-specific (BBC 2005: 20). This demonstrates two divergent approaches. One begins with the objective of serving the wider public, irrespective of varying levels of adoption and use. The BBC's guidelines for designing iTV services are explicitly inclusive in this respect: 'The audience of our services is diverse. All services should be easy to use for the audience, from the young through to the elderly. One in 30 of our audience has a visual impairment.' (BBC 2005: 2)

In this way, it is possible to identify new audiences and uses of iTV which can then be grown in the future. The second approach takes as its departure point what is already known about traditional broadcast television audiences and applies this genre/gender classification to the design of iTV services. That is, by understanding the well-established patterns by which people watch television, interactive features designed for particular audiences like women have a better chance of being adopted and subsequently, for channels to receive a return on investment. For example, knowledge of how women use video cassette recorders provides a model for how iTV services like video-on-demand or personal video recorders could successfully cater for female markets (Gawlinski 2003: 213). Furthermore, this means that possibilities are not constrained by having to design for universal access (ibid. 215).

A feminist approach to designing iTV services acknowledges women as vital to the growth of iTV markets and responds accordingly to the gender gaps which currently exist in the development and consumption of iTV. In short, it argues that the consideration of gender in the design of iTV experiences should be paramount. 'An interactive television service designed purely for usability may allow viewers to perform tasks, but risks leaving them feeling disconnected, uninvolved and without a sense of allegiance.' (Gawlinski 2003: 201)

Experience design with a feminist orientation understands that utility and usability are not sufficient to engage women in the adoption and use of iTV. Rather, a sense of affiliation with a community must be provided as well as opportunities to share experiences with others. This means giving women a voice through which they can contribute feedback and exercise control over how they represent themselves. It is about building capacity for personal and emotional connection in addition to the personalization of communal experience: '... the medium is ripe for projects that take advantage of iTV's potential to create a more personal, relevant experience...' (Curran 2003: 20)

There are now pay TV channels orientated to female audiences, such as Arena, Hallmark and Channel W, with the occasional interactive application for their programming, such as one associated with the *Sex and the City* series. This asked questions of the audience in regard to the plot and characters.

In contrast to fictional lives and people, talk shows often appeal to the 'reality' of women's existence and feminine cognitive styles of being 'artistic, sensitive, integrated, deep, intersubjective, empathic, associative, affective, open, personalised, aesthetic and receptive' (Humm 1989: 85). The genre has the potential to faciliate a sense of community connection and participation. The online domain has surpassed iTV in this respect, with social networking sites such as MySpace and Facebook that allow women to reach out to friends, join groups and generate networks of similar interest. Yet there are few examples of iTV enhancements that have been developed for this genre (Lu 2005: 72) which would further contribute to a 'politics of the personal', despite that in the free-to-air (FTA) TV channels, women are traditionally targeted with morning talk shows.

In the niche channel environment of pay TV, interactive experiences developed for women focus on topics that are traditionally feminine such as horoscopes, cooking and decorating. Such superficial attempts to feminize iTV, combined with the absence of interactive enhancements to popular female genres such as drama and talk shows, are indicative of the iTV industry's failure to understand female audiences. It confirms Lu's (2005: 184) contention that in 'the design of iTV applications, the user-centred approach is rarely practiced'.

The lack of success of iTV applications aimed at women needs to be read in the context of what female audiences are prepared to invest in. The increasing subscriptions to pay TV channels such as Arena, Hallmark and W, as well as decreasing free-to-air audiences suggest that women are prepared to part with their money for content targeted especially at them. Any interactive applications or services (such as voting or competitions) offered with these respective channels generally incur additional costs. But only by requiring payment and user-authorization, can such enhancements be effectively measured. In other words, a 'return path' from the user's set top box back to the broadcaster is necessary before any kind of degree of success or popularity can be calculated. However, there are also many iTV applications that are free, do not have an associated charge and do not need a 'return path': by what criteria can these be evaluated given that there is no way for the broadcaster to know whether they are being used and how frequently? This is unlike the evaluation of websites which can offer detailed reporting on site traffic, unique visits and page hits. By contrast, iTV channels seem to invest in the development of interactive features without similar means to gauge their performance. The time and effort to design and produce an iTV application may be easily wasted: if the sponsor does not immediately see a high response rate, they will not repeat the exercise.

Therefore, it is likely that much iTV consumption by women is largely 'invisible' in that they may be using applications which are free and do not require a 'return path'. This invisibility means that supposed 'unsuccessful' ventures such as *Fat Cow Motel*, an interactive soap opera on Australian television, have to be questioned. That is, its apparent lack of success may not be due to minimal uptake or use, but rather the difficulty of measuring uptake or use. It is difficult to conclude from such data that 'women are not interested in iTV'. Their under-representation as iTV consumers is comparable to women bearing the bulk of unpaid activity in the economy, in that they are engaged in work that is unacknowledged and unquantifiable (Baker 2007). Women may be highly active participants in iTV but it is just not seen.

As the key financial decision-makers in households, women are not only subscribing to pay TV for their families, but for themselves. Given that they are willing to be targeted through 'women's channels', the logical extension of this niche programming is personalization, whereby the broadcaster can target households or individuals through tailored messages sent to the viewer's set top box, and viewers will be able to revisit programmes outside of broadcast times or see unedited versions. Personal video recorders (PVRs) such as TiVO are an example of this, allowing users to bookmark programmes and based on this, predicts and records content that the user may like. TiVO also enables users to select movies according to actor, look up all the roles they have played, browse through their photo galleries, as well as filter results by genre. The obligations of women's unpaid work (such as cooking, cleaning and childcare) means that the ability to 'timeshift', to interact with a programme in a flexible manner, is personally appealing and relevant to women. This includes being able to pause and rewind live broadcasts, skip advertisements, in addition to scheduling recordings online (and not just using the remote control). This type of interactivity can be defined as 'female-friendly' in that has been designed with consideration to women's emotional role as primary carers and homemakers. As Halleck (1991: 227) maintains, technologies create communities of interest, and women must be considered in this balancing act between social equity and digital content. 'Television is a shared and gendered medium; so is video' (Silverstone 1990: 179).

Summary

- New technological experiences such as iTV ought to be designed with an inclusive outlook that considers the wider community as well as communities of interest.
- Designers need to be wary of gender imbalances in modes of production, representation and consumption of interactive experiences – particularly where technologies are still in early stages of adoption.
- In designing women's interactions with new technologies such as iTV, an understanding of women's experiences with preceding technologies and how these are appropriated in their everyday lives is necessary.
- Feminist approaches to experience design privilege the personal and emotional, appealing to feminine cognitive styles of being 'artistic, sensitive, integrated, deep, intersubjective, empathic, associative, affective, open, personalised, aesthetic and receptive' (Humm 1989: 85).
- Designers must take into account the constraints on women's time resulting from them bearing a disproportionate amount of unpaid work.

References and *recommended reading

Baehr, H. and Dyer, G. (eds) (1987), *Boxed In: Women and Television*. London: Pandora.

Baker, K. (2007), 'The problem with unpaid work', *University of St Thomas Law Journal*, Social Science Research Network [Online] Available: http://ssrn.com/abstract=996161. Accessed June 28 2007.

*BBC (2005), *Designing for Interactive Television v1.0: BBCi and Interactive TV Programmes*. London: British Broadcasting Corporation.

Caine, B., Gatens, M., Grahame, E., Larbalestier, J., Watson, S. and Webby, E. (1998), *Australian Feminism: A Companion*. Melbourne. Oxford University Press.

Curran, S. (2003), *Convergence Design: Creating the User Experience for Interactive Television, Wireless and Broadband*. Gloucester: Rockport.

Dyer, G. (1987), 'Women and television: an overview', in H. Baehr and G. Dyer (eds), *Boxed In: Women and Television*. London: Pandora.

Eronen, L. (2002), 'Design of interactive television programmes', *CHINZ 2002 Proceedings of the 3rd Annual ACM SIGCHI-NZ Symposium on Computer-Human Interaction*. Hamilton, New Zealand. 11–12 July, pp. 73–78.

Gawlinski, M. (2003), *Interactive Television Production*. Oxford: Focal Press.

Glaessner, V. (1990), 'Gendered fictions', in A. Goodwin and G. Whannel (eds), *Understanding Television*. London: Routledge.

Halleck, D. (1991), 'Watch out Dick Tracy! Popular video in the wake of *Exxon Valdez*', in C. Penley and A. Ross (eds), *Technoculture*. Minneapolis: University of Minnesota Press.

HREOC (2000), 'Bruce Lindsay Maguire v. Sydney Organizing Committee for the Olympic Games', *Human Rights and Equal Opportunity Commission: Disability Rights* [Online] Available: http://www.hreoc.gov.au/disability_rights/decisions/comdec/2000/DD000120.htm. Accessed August 6 2008.

*Humm, M. (1989), *The Dictionary of Feminist Theory*. New York: Prentice Hall.

Hyman, P. (2004) '"Casual" video games are serious business', *The Hollywood Reporter*, [Online] Available: http://www.hollywoodreporter.com/hr/search/article_display.jsp?vnu_content_id=1000535245. Accessed August 6 2008.

Jackson, S. (1993), *Women's Studies: Essential Readings*. New York: NYU Press.

Kaplan, E. (1983), *Women and Film*. London: Methuen.

Kendall, L. (1999), 'Recontextualising "cyberspace": Methodological considerations for online research', in S. Jones (ed.), *Doing Internet Research*. London: Sage.

Leung, L. (2005), *Virtual Ethnicity: Race, Resistance and the World Wide Web*. Aldershot: Ashgate.

Lu, K. (2005) 'Interaction design principles for interactive television', Master of Science in Information Design and Technology thesis, Georgia Institute of Technology [Online] Available: http://idt.gatech.edu/ms_projects/klu/lu_karyn_y_200505_mast.pdf. Accessed August 6 2008.

Mann, P. (1989), 'Portrayal of women in advertising: Self-regulation and other options', *Media Information Australia*, 51, February.

Mulvey, L. (1989), *Visual and Other Pleasures*. London: Macmillan.

Mumby, D. and Putnam, L. (1992), 'The politics of emotion: A feminist reading of bounded rationality', *Academy of Management Review*, 17, pp. 465–86.

Nakamura, L. (2002), *Cybertypes: Race, Ethnicity and Identity on the Internet*. New York: Routledge.

Nightingale, V. (1990), 'Women as audiences', in M. Brown (ed.), *Television and Women's Culture*. Sydney: Currency.

Norman, D. (2004), *Emotional Design*. New York: Basic Books.

Radway, J. (1984), *Reading the Romance: Woman, Patriarchy and Popular Literature*. Chapel Hill: University of North Caroline Press.

Roy Morgan Research Pty Ltd (January to December 2006) 'Interest in watching sports on payTV'. Melbourne: Roy Morgan Single Source Australia.

Silverstone, R. (1990), 'Television and everyday life: Towards an anthropology of the television audience', in M. Ferguson (ed.), *Public Communication: the New Imperatives*. London: Sage, pp.173–89.

Stanley, L. (ed.) (1990), *Feminist Praxis: Research, Theory and Epistemology in Feminist Sociology*. London: Routledge.

Tunstall, J. (1993) *Television Producers*. London: Routledge.

Williamson, J. (1978), *Decoding Advertisments: Ideology and Meaning in Advertising*. London: Marion Boyars.

7

LESSONS FROM WEB ACCESSIBILITY AND INTELLECTUAL DISABILITY

Helen Kennedy and Linda Leung

The aim of this chapter is to map out why considering the needs of intellectually disabled communities might be beneficial to digital experience designers. It does this by addressing the question: what can digital experience designers learn from the field of web accessibility and intellectual disability? We do this first through a discussion of what intellectual disability is, which is followed by an examination of the accessibility requirements of this varied community and how these requirements might be addressed. Following this, we present some case studies of intellectually disabled web users and reflect on what these examples reveal about the design of online experiences. We conclude with some suggestions about what this area can contribute to the field of digital experience design.

What is intellectual disability?

Census data collected by governments indicate that approximately 20 per cent of the population in countries such as Australia and the UK have a disability. This may be physical, sensory, intellectual, psychiatric, neurological, a learning disability or result from a physical disfigurement or the presence in the body of disease-causing organisms (World Health Organization 1980). Because this is based on self-reporting – that is, acknowledgement and declaration of one's own disability – this proportion is considered to be an underestimate. Furthermore, legal definitions of disability as stated in Disability Discrimination Acts are generally broader than those specified in data. This means that more than 20 per cent of populations could be described as having a disability and suggests that the prevalence of disability cannot be ignored.

When it comes to the kind of disability that is the focus of this chapter, intellectual disability, the first hurdle to understanding its nature and scope is that definitions of intellectual disability vary across history and geography, and the term is often used interchangeably with cognitive disability and learning disability. The same 'condition' has different labels in different countries: in the UK, it is mainly referred to as learning disability. In the US, learning disability is understood to refer to scholastic disability – what might be defined as learning difficulties in the UK. Thus, the term developmental disability is preferred in the US. Internationally, the term intellectual disability is used, and, as this is also the term recommended by the World Health Organization (WHO), this is what we adopt in this chapter.

An intellectual disability is a condition that affects a person's intellectual, social and emotional development. Intellectual disabilities take many forms and have many effects. Generally, a child with an intellectual disability will learn more slowly than other children of the same age. Some have difficulty communicating or socializing; others have problems with activities like reading, writing and mathematics. Other intellectually disabled people have trouble controlling their emotions or behaviour. The WHO and United Nations (UN) defines 'mental retardation', another interchangeable term, as consisting of an IQ of less than 70, coupled with low levels of social and communication function, whose onset, critically, must be congenital or in early years. What is important for our purposes here is to note that the category of 'intellectual disability' encompasses a wide range of conditions, each with its own set of accessibility requirements. Indeed, when Helen started researching intellectual disability and web accessibility with the Rix Centre for Innovation and Learning Disability at the University of East London in the UK, the centre's director felt that, given the complexity and diversity of intellectual disability, this was better experienced than explained, and he sent her off to a couple of Special Education Needs (SEN – another interchangeable term) educational institutions. This was his approach with all new collaborators at Rix – a baptism by fire, which proved extremely effective in transmitting an understanding of what intellectual disability is.

It is claimed that 20 per cent of children will have an intellectual disability at some time in their lives, which may result from medical problems, sensory impairments, physical disabilities, emotional and behavioural difficulties, language impairments, or specific learning problems such as dyslexia or autism (Emerson et al. 2001: 7). For example, a child with an ear infection may be temporarily hearing impaired, affecting their ability to listen and learn in a classroom setting. Alternatively, a child's learning may also be disrupted by the emotional upheaval associated with relocation, divorce or death of a family member. People with intellectual disabilities often also have related sensory or motor disabilities.

That disability affects such as large proportion of general populations suggests that designing to accommodate the needs of people with disabilities should simply be a part and parcel, rather than an anomaly, of the design process. In recent years, accessibility has been embraced by web designers as a result of new policy and legislation, more accessible tools and its acceptance by web design gurus. It has been embraced for a number of reasons. First, there is the numbers/

business argument proposed above: that people with disabilities are significant in number and therefore form a substantial potential market. Second, there is the moral/ethical case: that is, if you design an online experience that is targeted at the general public, then your design should be accessible to all. Third (and this has perhaps been the most persuasive argument for many designers) is the proposal that 'accessibility is a matter of usability' (Clarke 2006: 12). To elaborate on the words of web design guru Andy Clarke: '...we should be designing our content so it is globally accessible and meets the needs of as many people as is possible and practical given our specific circumstances, regardless of their abilities or the type of device they choose to access the Web' (ibid. 12).

In addition, experience designers should note that environments, whether physical, digital or virtual, can enable or disable. A building which can only be entered via steps turns reliance on a wheelchair, zimmerframe or pram into a disability. It is a form of design which excludes those who use these technologies. A ramp, in lieu of stairs, exemplifies inclusive design which minimizes disability, as it does not adversely impact on either wheelchair, zimmerframe and pram users, nor those who do not rely on these technologies. In terms of digital design, experiences should be as accessible to those who do not see, hear, move, communicate or read well, as those who do. This is called a social model of disability, as opposed to a medical model. In the latter, the disability is the individual's problem, which needs to be 'fixed'. In the former, it is society that is disabling, and by changing, adapting and modifying society, and aspects of society like buildings or the World Wide Web, to be inclusive, the world within which disabled communities live can become more enabling. The World Health Organization (2001) recognizes that it is the environment, not the person, which is responsible for the difficulties experienced in having participation restricted or activities limited. Emerson et al. sum up this position as follows: 'A social model of disability defines it as social restriction or oppression imposed by non-disabled others and advocates the removal of socially constructed barriers' (Emerson et al. 2001: 19).

Such a view empowers digital experience designers, because it tells us that digital environments can be made differently. They do not necessarily need to exclude; by understanding and attending to the needs of disabled users, they can also include.

Accessible design, usable design, experience design
The World Wide Web Consortium (W3C) promotes the design of such inclusive environments and experiences through its Web Accessibility Initiative (WAI) and its Web Content Accessibility Guidelines (WCAG). As World Wide Web founder Tim Berners-Lee claims, 'the power of the Web is in its universality. Access by everyone regardless of disability is an essential aspect'. However, the initiative originally concentrated its efforts on the needs of people with motor and sensory impairments. For example, it recommended that auditory and visual content on web pages should also be represented in textual form to be accessible to visually impaired users with assistive devices such as screen readers. Thus while these guidelines have been enshrined in law internationally, intellectual disability advocates and lobbyists feel that they do not adequately address the specific access needs of the intellectually disabled community.

Accessibility guidelines specific to people with intellectual disabilities are said to be 'almost non-existent' (Harrysson et al. 2004). Sensory impairments, particularly hearing and vision, are also common in people with learning disabilities, more so than in the general population (Emerson et al. 2001: 27). However, this group are mostly not readers and experience difficulties in understanding the written and spoken word. Visually rich media is more accessible than text to people with intellectual disabilities, while the opposite is true for people with vision impairment. Thus the spoken-text alternatives to website content which might work for people who are visually impaired are not so accessible for people with intellectual disabilities. Under existing W3C guidelines, 'rich media' which incorporates sound, imagery, video and animation to make content meaningful for an intellectually disabled user is deemed inaccessible without alternative text-based formats.

The W3C WAI has attempted to respond to criticism of the limitations of existing documents in relation to intellectual disability in version 2 of their guidelines, currently in working draft form (http://www.w3.org/TR/WCAG20), which is a positive step. However, a number of intellectual disability interest groups registered their concern with the W3C's claim in an earlier draft that compliance with WCAG2 would ensure meeting the needs of disabled groups, including those with intellectual disabilities. This led to a revision to this claim, which now states that some of the accessibility needs of this group are met in the guidelines, but not all, and that more research is needed in this area. Clearly, then, it is not the case that adhering to the guidelines will mean that web environments are accessible to people with intellectual disabilities. In turn, this suggests that other approaches to inclusive experience design, not just guidelines-based, is needed. This is the focus of current research in which Helen is engaged on the project Inclusive New Media Design, which aims to identify the best way to encourage web designers and developers to build sites accessible to people with intellectual disabilities (http://www.inclusivenewmedia.org).

As many people with intellectual disabilities also have physical impairments which affect mobility and speech, they often have limited social networks, even though they rate friendship highly (Emerson et al. 2001: 22). Thus, online environments potentially become important social networking tools. For those with language difficulties, speech therapists acknowledge the vital role of 'quality of personal relationship, the opportunities the person has to use his/her communication skills' in improving a person's ability to communicate (ibid. 32). Video telephony has been found to be a successful platform for developing the social networks of those with intellectual disabilities (Renblad 2000). Thus, information and communication technologies can be used to overcome some of these disabilities by offering 'inclusion of youngsters and children with disabilites in the school-of-all and in the life-of-all' (Besio and Salminen 2004: 115).

Research shows that the leisure pursuits of those with intellectual disabilities tend to be solitary (Emerson et al. 2001: 48). Activities such as listening to music or watching videos are consistent with the often individualistic nature of computer use and online interaction. Thus, the design of online experiences associated with these activities ought to consider people with intellectual disabilities as part of their audience. At the same time as and in contrast to such solitary pursuits, other activities, such as going shopping, are often dependent on the assistance of family members. Indeed, having an intellectual disability usually means some degree of reliance on the assistance of others to perform those functions and activities that are part of daily life (Grove et al. 1999). In cases such as online shopping, the virtual realm serves as a platform for teaching someone how to do something (shopping online) in a context of communal computer use and interaction. This situation is also the case with parents or grandparents being coached in using the internet by their children and grandchildren. Therefore, experience designers need to consider the role and necessity of human mediation and support when designing online interactions, as they may be experienced communally.

The self-advocacy movement within intellectual disability communities encourages every intellectually disabled person to be enabled to exercise control over their own lives according to their capacity. Therefore, people with learning disabilities are encouraged to make decisions about:

- where to live
- with whom they live
- what they do during the day
- what to eat and drink
- where to work
- whether to become a parent
- whether to have medical or other treatment
- their finances (Emerson et al. 2001: 21).

Increasingly, the information that is sought to inform such decisions can be found online. Such information has the potential to give access to knowledge and imbue the user with power in their own decision-making (Hawkridge and Vincent 1992). This and the other examples cited above point to the many uses of online environments by intellectually disabled web users.

Of course, whether the resources to develop social networks, listen to music, watch videos, shop, find information to inform decision-making is accessible to people with intellectual disabilities is another question. According to Johnson and Hegarty (2003), dense text constitutes the majority of content for many websites. So how to remedy this? Emerson et al. (2001: 29) recommend that text should be augmented with signs or picture symbols to accommodate those who do not read well. A number of resources are available to assist designers in this. Internationally, Widgit 'software solutions of inclusion' (http://www.widgit.com) has developed a number of symbol-based products and resources to aid in communication for people with difficulties in this area. In the UK, Change Picture Bank (http://www.changepeople.co.uk), an equal rights organization for people with intellectual disabilities, have led the field in developing visual symbols which help to make information easier to understand.

Engagement and participation in online experiences are further enhanced for people with intellectual disabilities by the use of sound, photography, video, graphics and animation (Larcher 2000). Use of high quality visual and audio media serves to support, or in some cases, replace conventional linguistic forms such that heavy reliance on either textual or verbal instruction is reduced. This kind of 'multisensorial' design strategy can stimulate and heighten sensory response (Howes 2005: 3) and so maximize enjoyment of online experiences.

The concept of multisensorial design moves the field of online experience design from an emphasis on accessibility and usability to a focus on emotional, affective design. As highlighted above, a number of problems with existing accessibility advice have been identified in relation to intellectual disability accessibility. According to Kevin Carey, director of HumanITy: Inclusion in the Information Age (http://www.humanity.org.uk), a charity campaigning for the digital inclusion of disabled populations, a further problem with accessibility guidelines is their incredible complexity. This is coupled with what he defines as the 'excessive complexity of ICT design' which, according to Carey is 'an indulgence with which many users learn to live but [which] imposes massive additional disadvantages on disabled people'. Stripping away this unnecessary complexity, Carey argues that accessible design guidelines *can* be simple, and proposes the following three principles:

- Allow simplification and customization (that is, allow users to remove content unrelated to the task in hand).
- Create multi-modality (in other words, allow users to access content via the medium of their choice, be it textual, audio or visual).
- Allow user-interface choice (by this Carey means make content that works across platforms; see also Bywater 2005).

This simplification of advice on how to achieve inclusive experience design is indeed welcome. Other writers have taken a different approach to the problems associated with accessibility, however, and have moved the spotlight away from accessibility and usability to emotional design. An interesting case in point is Don Norman's recent book, *Emotional Design: Why we Love (or Hate) Everyday Things* (2004). Here Norman argues that the emotional side of design may be more important than the practical side. This is because aesthetically pleasing objects have a better chance of being adopted and used, because the user is better disposed towards them. Designers can therefore get away with more if a product is enjoyable. Norman reflects back on his own previous focus on usability and acknowledges that if we were to follow his previous prescriptions, our designs would all be usable, but ugly. Norman argues that there is a close relationship between cognition (which is cool and rational) and emotion (which is hot and irrational). Usability design as a field is rooted in cognitive science; as such, it fails to acknowledge the role of emotion (and its subconscious counterpart, affect) in human interactions with objects. Norman claims that emotion and affect are 'information-processing systems' which therefore need to be integral to the process of designing experiences. In highlighting the importance of emotion and affect, Norman points to what has been called 'the affective turn' in cultural studies, cultural theory and more generally – that is, a recognition of the role and importance of affective, bodily reactions and intensities in social experiences and interactions.

This relationship between cognition and emotion manifests itself in relation to intellectual disability in such a way that 'different' cognition makes for 'different' sensory responses, and limited cognition heightens sensory response; people with intellectual disabilities are doing the kind of multisensorial sensing that Howes (2005) argues for. Services providing care for people with intellectual disabilities use technologies to stimulate sensory responses, for example through hydrotherapy, touch-based sensory rooms or multimedia advocacy. In the latter cases, the use of multimedia by people with intellectual disabilities to facilitate communication about themselves and their preferences is often assumed to be purely representational, but it is also sensory, a kind of communication and memory augmentation based on sensory stimuli. In such instances, sensory channels are used to engage at a cognitive level. Such sensory stimulation sometimes means that people with intellectual disabilities display affective and disinhibited pleasure in the use of new technologies, as witnessed in the cases discussed below.

Another way of addressing the complex and diverse digital needs of people with intellectual disabilities is through personalization. After all, everyone, not just in intellectually disabled communities, is different, and what is effective experience design for one person may not be for another. Personalization can be defined in broad terms as the capacity of new media and ICTs to be adapted to meet the needs and desires of its individual users. Clearly, ICTs have a role to play in personalization practices, as they can provide the facility to:

■ identify appropriate content resources which can be modified, used and re-used
■ present a range of interfaces to learners, and
■ provide effective and adaptive assessment and reporting tools (BECTA 2005).

With intellectually disabled users, personalization clearly has its benefits, not only because it is a method by which to respond to difference and diverse accessibility needs, but also because something like a photograph of a user which is presented to him or her as s/he accesses a system contributes to this user's sense of self and self-worth (Bunning and Heath forthcoming). Nonetheless, there are obstacles to achieving personalization, as Helen found on a research project which developed a personalized web-based system for intellectually disabled users. These included:

■ resourcing (including difficulties with operating technology, technological malfunction, lack of equipment and resources to support the use of equipment, lack of institutional technical support and strategic approaches to training teachers in the use of ICTs)
■ managing the differing expectations of different parties
■ issues relating to the paucity of age-appropriate content for this community
■ constraints imposed by the 'accountability culture' of the educational context in which we were researching, and
■ different understandings of what it means to 'do personalization' (see Kennedy 2008).

Further, as journalist and IT consultant, David Walker points out that personalization has not been well implemented in many websites, the success of Amazon being atypical. He argues that because personalization is costly, dependent on user-data and often driven by technology which understands users poorly: 'Internet personalisation is not a Big Idea but a Small Idea, a Special-Circumstances Idea, a Use-With-Care Idea. It is an idea that most Web sites should, for now, dismiss' (Walker 2000).

User testing websites with people with disabilities has been described as extreme user testing. This is because disabled users tend to identify more problems than able users. Following on from this, if a website can be made to work for disabled-user testers, it is usually safe to assume that it will work for all users. Meeting the complex and diverse accessibility and usability needs of people with intellectual disabilities presents a further challenge to designing inclusive new media for people with physical disabilities; user testing with this group could be defined as extremely extreme user testing. Thus carrying out user testing with physically and intellectually disabled users can prove extremely fruitful to the online experience designer. So let us now consider those users a little more closely.

Case studies

Here we present some case studies of web use by users with intellectual disabilities, in order to reflect on what such examples reveal about the design of online experiences. These are not intended to illustrate to experience designers what it is like to have an intellectual disability, but rather, the highly affective and disinhibited responses of people with intellectual disabilities when using multimedia technologies. The video ethnographies upon which the first two cases are based formed part of Project @pple, a research initiative which aimed to explore and evaluate the terms on which people with intellectual disabilities can participate in the web. Video clips can be found at: http://www.thebigtree.org/roots/html/projectapple/personas. htm (Cases 1 and 4). The third case study refers to a student project which can be accessed at: http://www.trans-active.co.uk/teenz/theden/html/bed1.htm (click on the graphic of the stereo to visit the music zone).

Case 1

Astley[*] is in a busy and chaotic classroom. Initially, Astley demonstrates rather unfocused behaviour. The teacher tells the researcher 'you won't get much sense out of Astley I'm afraid' and tells Astley to put his shoes back on. However, he soon becomes intently focused on the task he sets himself using the PC, mouse and keyboard. He does a Google search, typing 'www.cops.com' into the text box, clicking the search button, and rapidly scanning up and down the text results. Dissatisfied with what is displayed, he clicks the images button on the Google homepage and scans down the page of thumbnails that results. A few minutes later, he locates a web page which features the tune for which he was searching and dances to the track in his seat. He is enjoying the web page but gets frustrated when his clicking of the mouse causes dialogue boxes to pop up on screen. He becomes angry with the computer and says 'Don't say that! What's wrong with you?'

---

[*] Real names are not used.

Case 2

Fourteen-year old Amina,* who does not have conventional language and has quite profound and complex intellectual and physical disabilities, uses a touchscreen monitor to play a computer game in which animal shapes that float across the screen disappear when touched. They also emit an audio effect as the action occurs. As she successfully completes each phase of the game through laboured physical movements, the words 'excellent' and brilliant' appear on her screen in a large font. She is assisted by her class teacher who encourages and supports her by reading out the reward messages on screen, clapping at her achievements and exclaiming 'well done!' Amina appears to be very pleased with her achievements on the computer.

Case 3

A group of undergraduate students create some web content for a website aimed at teenagers with intellectual disabilities and their able peers. The students take very seriously the 'nothing about us without us' ethos of the self-advocacy movement within intellectually disabled communities and carry out admirably thorough user testing. They produce an interactive web space akin to a teenager's bedroom, where clicking on various items in the room take you to different games. Clicking on the stereo takes you to the music zone, in which you can click on the space bar to make a range of different figures do dance moves, and changes the colours of the disco lights. The user testing session is an emotional one, as the teenagers whoop and jump up and down with delight at the effect of their interactions with the computer, and the students glow with pride at their ability to make something, albeit unpolished, that really works for their users.

For people whose cognitive hard-wiring is different and other, there is little room for anything other than media-rich experience design. These examples set out the case for emotional, affective, media-rich approaches in the design of online experiences for people with intellectual disabilities. This can be seen in the highly affective and disinhibited responses of people with intellectual disabilities when using multimedia technologies. Astley exemplifies visceral and 'gut' reaction to a self-directed task, as do the teenagers in their music session. Astley shows himself to be very able in his web search, and his reaction to the content he locates communicates his pleasure very clearly. At the same time, he does not disrupt the class as he focuses on his activity, even when he becomes angry. Amina's slow and careful physical interaction with the touchscreen is also visceral, albeit less energetic than the other users discussed here. It also differs from the others in that it is assisted. In Amina's case, touch is both a motor ability and a sensory capacity through which she communicates her understanding of her teacher's encouraging words and the purpose of the game itself. Hearing and vision are other senses which are mobilized through auditory and visual content by Amina and the group of teenagers, and the animated movement in the games they are playing combines with this to capture their attention in a way that textual content simply could not. Amina's resulting gestures of delight are indicators of her sensory pleasure in her engagement with the computer. Likewise, Astley's seated dancing and the teenagers' whooping and jumping is another example of the kind of disinhibited response to multimedia experiences sometimes displayed by people with intellectual disabilities. People with intellectual disabilities are necessarily more sensory; their cognitive limitations lead them to experience and communicate on a more affective level. The emotional character of their engagement with machines needs to be regarded as an accessibility and usability issue in inclusive online design.

Observation of people with intellectual disabilities interacting with new technologies suggests that there is a need to rethink the term 'disability'. Those who seem significantly disabled in terms of communication and cognition show themselves to be rather more able when it comes to technology use. This suggests that disability is contingent: someone disabled in one context may be very able in another. It also suggests the usefulness of a model of disability which recognizes that environments, virtual or otherwise, can be disabling or can be constructed in ways which are enabling.

Summary
In conclusion, what can digital experience designers learn from the field of web accessibility and intellectual disability? Our suggestions are summarized below.

- Acknowledge the breadth of disability: 20 per cent of the population in countries such as Australia and the United Kingdom have a disability of which learning disability is only one kind.
- Designing for intellectual disability means designing for users who have difficulty comprehending the spoken and written word: do this by augmenting text with signs or picture symbols.
- Simplify, customize and personalize, but recognize that this difficult to implement well.
- The notion of 'experience' is open to interpretation, and experiences are diverse. What is an experience? It's different for different people; and for users with learning disabilities, it is necessarily multisensorial.
- Design online experiences that are media-rich, affective and highly sensory.
- Do extreme user testing on users with both physical and intellectual disabilities.
- Design online experiences which allow for the possibility of non-isolated/supported engagement with online environments.

References and *recommended reading

BECTA (British Educational Communications and Technology Agency) (2005), *Personalised Learning and ICT* [Online] Available: http://foi.becta.org.uk/display.cfm?cfid=662527&cftoken=63d05f972 705-4B7DF789-C05D-EAE1-98481165EA7BBC6B&resID=14738. Accessed August 6 2008.

Besio, S. and Salminen, A. (2004), 'Children and youngsters and technology', *Technology and Disability*, 16, pp. 115–17.

Bunning, K. and Heath, R. (forthcoming), 'The advocacy process in young people with intellectual disability: a place for ICT and rich and multiple media?', *Journal of Applied Research in Intellectual Disabilities*.

Bywater, B. (2005), 'Accessibility design guidelines can be simple', *UsabilityNews.com* [Online] Available: http://www.usabilitynews.com/news/article2485.asp. Accessed August 6 2008.

*Change Picture Bank [Online] Available: http://www.changepeople.co.uk. Accessed August 6 2008.

Clarke, A. (2006), *Transcending CSS: the Fine Art of Web Design*, Berkeley: New Riders.

Emerson, E., Hatton, C., Felce, D. and Murphy, G. (2001), *Learning Disabilities – the Fundamental Facts*. London: The Foundation for People with Learning Disabilities.

Grove, N., Bunning, K., Porter, J. and Olsson, C. (1999), 'See what I mean: interpreting the meaning of communication by people with severe and profound intellectual disabilities', *Journal of Applied Research in Intellectual Disabilities*, 12, pp. 190–203.

Harrysson, B., Svensk, A. and Johansson, G. (2004) 'How people with developmental disabilities navigate the internet', *British Journal of Special Education*, 31: 3, pp. 138–42.

Hawkridge, D. and Vincent, T. (1992), *Learning Difficulties and Computers: Access to the Curriculum*. London: Jessica Kingsley.

Howes, D. (2005), 'Architecture of the senses', *Sense of the City Exhibition Catalogue*. Montreal: Canadian Centre for Architecture [Online] Available: http://www.david-howes.com/DH-research-sampler-arch-senses.htm. Accessed August 6 2008.

*HumanITy [Online] Available: http://www.humanity.org.uk. Accessed August 6 2008.

*Inclusive New Media Design [Online] Available: http://www.inclusivenewmedia.org. Accessed August 6 2008.

Johnson, R. and Hegarty, J. (2003), 'Websites as educational motivators for adults with learning disability', *British Journal of Educational Technology*, 34: 4, pp. 479–86.

Kennedy, H. (2008), 'New media's potential for personalisation', *Information, Communication and Society*, 11: 3 (April), pp. 307–25.

Larcher, J. (2000), 'Information technology for children with language difficulties', in W. Rinaldi (ed.), *Language Difficulties in an Educational Context*. London: Whurr Publishers, pp. 131–47.

Norman, D. (2004), *Emotional Design: Why we Love (or Hate) Everyday Things*. New York: Basic Books.

Renblad, K. (2000), 'Persons with intellectual disability and their opportunities to exert influence in their activities and social contacts: An interview study', *Technology and Disability*, 13, pp. 55–65.

Walker, D. (2000), 'Personalisation goes one-on-one with reality', *Shorewalker.com* [Online] Available: http://www.shorewalker.com/section1/personalisation_worth.html. Accessed August 6 2008.

Widgit Software [Online] Available: http://www.widgit.com. Accessed August 6 2008.

World Health Organization (1980), International Classification of Functioning, Disability and Health. Geneva: WHO.

World Health Organization (2001) International Classification of Functioning, Disability and Health (ICF) [Online] Available: http://www.who.int/classifications/icf/en/. Accessed August 6 2008.

*World Wide Web Consortium (2004), 'Web Accessibility Initiative' [Online] Available: http://www.w3.org/WAI. Accessed August 6 2008.

*World Wide Web Consortium (2004), 'Web Content Accessibility guidelines 2.0' [Online] Available: http://www.w3.org/TR/WCAG20. Accessed August 6 2008.

8

Beyond the Visual: Applying Cinematic Sound Design to the Online Environment

Mark Ward and Linda Leung

Cinema is an alchemical interaction between its three constituent elements of sound, visuals and story. To be 'cinematic' is to combine these elements in ways that make the impact of the resulting experience larger than the sum of its parts. A movie might have lush production design and lighting, lyrical camerawork, sensual soundscape or an engaging story, but in a 'cinematic' work these distinctions tend to recede to give way to an overarching feeling of salient wholeness. The 'cinematic' experience seems to defy dissection – to talk about one element is difficult without talking about all other elements – and it is this level of consolidation to which digital designers aspire when creating user experiences. Over time, cinema has refined the ability to design such holistic experiences, which seduce and immerse its audiences into the filmic world, engaging them emotionally and convincing them to suspend their disbelief.

However, while the mechanisms of engagement and immersion have been studied extensively in terms of story and visual image, the role of sound has enjoyed less attention in film theory. In spite of this theoretical blind spot, the film industry has nevertheless created an entire discipline of sound design. By comparison, the consideration of sound in particular types of digital interactive experiences is still in its infancy, perhaps equivalent to cinema's 'silent' era. Therefore, what can designers for computer screens learn from techniques of the silver screen in terms of sound design? How might sound contribute to the emotional life of digital interactive experiences as it does to a film?

In this chapter, we compare the development of sound design in cinema with that of digital interactive environments, ranging from computer systems to CD-ROMs to websites. Along the way, we examine the types of sonic problem-solving and conceptual tools used by film-makers in the hope that digital designers need not reinvent, but rather benefit from a century's cinematic sound practices.

Loud and clear: Making the historical case for sound

After a century of cinema how can it be that sound design continues to operate in an almost theory-free vacuum? The language and vocabulary of sound is not as sophisticated as for the moving image, and yet sound informs and anchors the moving image. Film is an *audio*-visual (AV) medium. In the term 'AV', audio precedes the visual: that is, not only is sound integral, it is prioritized. This reflects the developmental history of media, whereby the rise of radio and recorded music industries meant that audiences were already well-practiced at mediated listening before their initiation into film.

Early cinema is commonly perceived as 'silent' (and thus a visual medium only) because no sound information was printed upon the filmstrip. In fact, a vast array of aural strategies were marshalled around the projected visual image, with many valiant but failed attempts to synchronize picture and sound (Abel and Altman 2001). For example, specific scores were composed and 'effects men' – even troupes of actors – were employed to provide a live accompaniment to the vision track. There was Thomas Edison and Eduard Muuybridge's joint venture that sought to fuse Muuybridge's moving-image system with Edison's gramophone. In pursuit of the holy grail of a single system of sound and image projection, competing systems appeared such as Edison's Kinetophone (which appeared first in 1895 and then in a re-designed form in 1913) and Gaumonts' Chronophone (1902). These proposed technology solutions to synchronizing sound with image were expensive, with theatrical venues reluctant to install costly sound replay systems, while a myriad of non-standardized equipment locked exhibitors into proprietary systems that reproduced sound of low quality. To place film sound in this historical and technological context goes a long way to explaining why early cinema has been theorized as an intrinsically silent visual medium.

From this vantage point, similarities with the practice of sound design in digital interactive experiences become apparent. As in the beginnings of cinema, early online experiences of sound have been contained within the boundaries of the lowest technical denominator. Until relatively recently, the online experience was often disturbed by buffer under-runs and visual stutter, streaming video that displayed picture and sound out of sync, and poor sound quality due to bandwidth and compression issues. All of these instances are analogues of problems faced in cinema's early development. Likewise, digital experience designers could not rely on the availability of appropriate technology for the distribution of sound. Therefore, the biases of cinema in privileging sight over hearing, and in being predisposed to visual dominance, have been repeated in digital interactive (and particularly online) media.

'The neglect of sound in mainstream interface design is striking. This can be partially accounted for by the lack of understanding about how sound is processed in the real world, and lack of inspiration about how to use sound innovatively.' (Macaulay et al. 2000: 161)

Early innovations in the use of sound in digital interactive environments were made by Apple Computer, which deployed personal computers into the marketplace equipped with sound-cards, as well as plug-in or built-in microphones allowing user-generated material to be recorded and manipulated, or linked to other documents. Most importantly, however, Apple's Macintosh user interface was conceived of in visual and aural terms, embedding William Gaver's work in auditory icons (1986) into its philosophical core.

If interactive media can be seen as part of the historical trajectory of cinema, its industries can adapt the lessons, rather than reproduce the mistakes, from the past in terms of sound design. To echo the promise of *The Jazz Singer* (the first commercially successful 'talking' film), 'You ain't heard nothin' yet'.

Sound and vision: How it works cognitively and experientially
Understanding how sound contributes to the emotional design of a film or digital interaction requires knowledge of the processes by which our senses gather data, translate this into perception, then make sense of those perceptions by integrating them into a coherent reality. The glue that binds this sensory data into perception, and then perception into narrative is emotion.

Emotion focuses us on a particular object or person. They are specific, controlling and do not allow for extended reasoning. Emotions are normally functional; that is, they tend toward producing an action, such as 'fight or flight' (Frijda cited in Tan 1996: 43–44). Emotions are dynamic, variable and very brief, lasting between two and eight seconds. Besides being short, they are intense, and unable to be altered whilst occurring. If the emotion system is sufficiently activated, the processed data will galvanize into a perception and percolate into our consciousness, thus becoming available to our attention (Tan 1996). This means that designers and film-makers have only a short amount of time to harness this emotional activation and engage their users and audience respectively.

In terms of evolution, dangerous and unpleasant experiences are more important to remember than pleasant ones, and so memories of our negative experiences are more strongly encoded, and therefore more easily recalled. A few brief seconds of intense emotion can set a mood lasting hours or even days. Film-makers have become adept at instigating negative emotions and setting black moods both intentionally (as in horror movies where uncomfortable feelings are deliberately triggered) and unintentionally (through poorly made films). Similarly, digital experience designers have been guilty of unconscious, negative emotional design, as in when users become frustrated by a DVD interface that is difficult to navigate or a website that is so disappointing that they refuse to return. As Donald Norman (2004: 119) asserts in his book, *Emotional Design*, sound can also harm an experience: noise, especially, is a source of negative affect. Indeed, in addition to negative emotional responses, noise also has the capacity to cause actual physical pain.

LeDoux (1998: 161–165) has described the pre-conscious processing of sound that occurs before it arrives in our awareness. Sound firstly reaches the 'ancient' part of the brain, the amygdala. This is a quick-and-dirty processor that allows reaction to a sound before it is 'heard'. It is a direct conduit to the emotions, capable of triggering the 'fight-or-flight' response. The sound also proceeds in parallel to the second processing centre, the relatively 'modern' auditory cortex. It takes twice as long to get to the cortex as it does to get to the amygdala. The auditory cortex 'listens' to what has been heard, employing cognitive scripts and ideas about what to do with the sound data. It is here the amygdala's response is either accepted or rejected. The effect of this double processing is that we emotionally *feel* a sound before we *know* we've heard it.

Paradoxically, sound is perceived in visual terms. In the 1990s, Neuman published results from a number of experiments conducted at MIT's Media Lab to determine the effects of sound quality on the perception of picture quality. The results of the experiments revealed that those watching standard resolution TV with CD-quality sound identified this combination as superior in visual quality to a system employing HD quality images with lo-fi sound (Neuman cited in Storms 1998).

Other examples of this cross-modal interaction can be seen in the work of cognitive psychologists Vroomen and de Gelder, who have conducted a multitude of experiments examining 'audio-visual fusion', a psychological mechanism whereby the modalities of hearing and vision fuse into one perception. Because of the principle psychologists call 'visual dominance', we perceive this fusion as essentially visual. Vroomen and de Gelder (2000) published findings of a series of experiments demonstrating the cross-modal influences of the auditory on the visual, drawing on the work of Sekular, Sekular and Lau (1997) where two groups of people were shown two discs of light, one moving left-to-right, and the other moving right-to-left so they seemed to pass through each other. Those who saw the discs mute saw the discs pass through each other. The group who saw the same visual action but with an auditory cue at the point where the discs overlap perceived the two discs to bounce off each other and travel back the way they came.

Another of Vroomen and de Gelder's (2004) experiments set up a series of light pulses accompanied by synchronized auditory cues. The subjects were to indicate when they became aware of the appearance of the visual flash. Whilst the visual sequence ran, the auditory bleeps were sped up or slowed down. The effect on perception was the sequence of visual flashes appeared to speed up and slow down in sympathy with the auditory cues. Both experiments demonstrate that sound controls and changes visual perception or what we think we see.

If sound design is a form of emotional or sensorial design, how can we describe its functions? While Chion (1994) and Holman (1997) have described a range of functions of sound on screen, we propose four that are particularly relevant to both film and interactive media:

1. Emotional truth
2. Point-of-view (Point-of-audition)
3. Storytelling
4. Physical experience

Arguably, the primary function of sound in both film and interactive media is the structuring and communicating of an **emotional truth**. Emotion is the prism through which all other information is filtered and so should be the guiding principle by which a work is created – that is, it is the organizing principle at the core of the work. This function harnesses the pre-attentional ability of sound to create mood, orienting the audience as to how visual information is to be received or interpreted. It is the key that the audience uses to make sense or meaning, and a tool for the user to check the veracity of the message they are receiving. It happens before rational logic, is pre-conscious and visceral and therefore has the capacity to affect us in a primal way.

Sound sets emotion, which in turn, sets mood. Mood can be described as a general state of mind without reference to a particular object. Mood is not directly connected with actions, and is more passive and basic than emotion. Mood is a more stable and longer-lasting process than emotion, allowing us to orient ourselves consistently to our environment without being on an 'emotional rollercoaster'. Mood smoothes things over, connecting our moment-to-moment existence so that the environment does not appear to be constantly changing around us. Mood is the afterglow of emotion, and it orients us toward experiencing the next similar emotion. As a result, mood sustains the likelihood of experiencing emotion, and the experience of emotion sustains mood (Smith 1999: 38, 111 – 114). Mood can be likened to the 'energy' of a film, or the 'feel' of a digital experience.

Sound also functions to establish **point-of-view**, or in this case **point-of-audition**. In film, point-of-audition has the role of simulating a character's feelings or thoughts by the choice of detail that is presented. Sound steers the audience through the available visual information, promoting what is important, and in which order. In a corporate website, this can be represented as the 'voice' of an organization, or as an acoustic environment or sense of place reflecting the 'buzz' of a company. Other digital experiences might allow sonic customization, whereby a user can self-select a mood, or express their taste or point-of-view, such as choosing either a male or female voice to provide spoken navigation instructions on an in-car GPS system.

The third function of sound is to structure storytelling. This is the case whether they are rich, complex stories as told in live-action film, or the simple, key messages of a web animation. Sound 'completes' the picture to legitimize it as a version of the real world; that is, it relates the screen-world to the offline world. It also acts as a form of grammar connecting or separating visual blocks to create new units of meaning. Sound has the role of a binding or unifying element, similar to connective tissue. This is also true in a cross-media sense, where a television advertising jingle, when used also in a website, can enable immediate cross-media recall and brand recognition.

The fourth and final function of sound is **physical experience**. It contributes to the overall multisensory experiences that are expected in cinema and, we argue, in interactive media. These are audio-visual media in which sound affects vision, and vision affects sound. In addition, digital media generally requires tactile interaction, and so encompasses touch as well. 'Hearing is a way of touching at a distance' (Schafer cited in Cranny-Francis 2005: 59).

This is where sound can have a synaesthetic role in interactive media, where sound is felt as much as it is heard, as can be seen in video games where explosive sounds and images are accompanied by vibrations in the console. That the senses of hearing and touch are so closely aligned provides a compelling argument for sound design to be a critical component of interactive (that is, tactile) media development.

An anatomy of sound design

Over the course of the last century, the design of sound in cinema has evolved into a specialized craft organized around four major aural categories:

- music
- ambient sound, or atmospheres
- sound effects
- dialogue (Murch, sound designer for *Apocalypse Now*, cited in Cranny-Francis 2005: 76)

Each of the above is deemed a discipline in its own right with its own artisans, spawning such roles as: production sound recordist, and boomswinger; ADR recordist (Automated Dialogue Replacement, otherwise known as 'post-sync dialogue'); foley artist and recordist; editors for dialogue, ADR, foley, effects and atmospheres; sound designer; composer; and sound mixer.

The role of **music** in creating a sense of space and place is already well known. Both Cubitt (1998: 97) and Bull (2000) liken music to architecture in terms of how it is used to structure daily life through the construction of acoustic space. In cinema, this additionally serves as a storytelling function, not only in helping to express the world within the film, but also by articulating the emotional status of characters. According to Norman (2004: 115), the affective states produced through music are cross-cultural: 'The proliferation of music speaks to the essential role it plays in our emotional lives. Music acts as a subtle subconscious enhancer of our emotional state throughout the day. This is why it is ever-present...' (Norman 2004: 119)

Thus, music operates at both macro and micro-levels of film. It can also be sub-categorized according to source (music from within the story-world), or score (music from outside the story-world). Likewise, this can be applied to the construction of online spaces, such as virtual worlds or corporate websites. A corporate website can be regarded as a world unto itself with its own characters or protagonists. Music is often part of the branding of large corporations in their broadcast media marketing (such as in advertising jingles), but is oftentimes overlooked in their online presence. Music has the capacity to maintain cross-media consistency in corporate branding as well as to quickly establish the qualities of a company's culture to the user. It is now also standard practice to highlight individuals and their roles within an organization on their website, and music can function as a signifier of the emotional life or 'vibe' of a company as well as the personalities of the people that work there.

This potential for music to affect experience lies in its impact on all three levels of brain processing:

1. Visceral in the initial pleasure of the rhythm, tune and sounds
2. Behavioural in the enjoyment of playing or listening
3. Reflective in the activity of analysing melody and lyrics (Norman 2004: 115).

Just as film scores can be enjoyed in their own right, digital interactive experiences can be similarly layered to allow music to take precedence over the visual image. Generally, a user can turn the sound on or off on a website: perhaps it should also be possible to fade or 'mute' the visual. Nonetheless, as is evident from film, when music is combined with the visual image in ways that also affect the brain viscerally, behaviorally and reflectively, deep and memorable experiences are evoked. When the brain is influenced on all these levels, it suspends its disbelief, accepting the differences between its own world and the new one created for it. The user is persuaded to stop, look and listen.

The world within a film is not only maintained through music, but also **sound effects** and **ambient sound**. These sonic elements may complement or contradict the objects or actions within the frame or, indeed, the entire filmic world. In one sense, these elements are designed to mimic or reflect the auditory landscape *in real life* (IRL), and thus to sustain the fiction of the world on the screen, aiding audiences to suspend their disbelief. On the other hand, sound effects may are also designed to comment upon and critique the film-world.

Sound effects for film are often described as 'hard effects' as they are sounds literally cut hard in sync with the picture. But the definition of sound effects stretches to also include *foley* and *atmospheres*. Foley is usually recorded in a sound studio to picture playback and usually refers to body movement, such as clothing, footsteps and other subtle motions. Foley is also a useful technique to record 'unnatural' sounds. It adds layers of 'reality' to actions or objects. Atmospheres, or ambient sounds, sonically represent the environment of the scene, such as distant traffic or wind through trees and telephone lines. Usually such ambient sounds contain information which construct and frame the emotional tone of the scene. All such sound can be 'real' or 'unreal' but most are not a literal translation of what one would hear in the visual location and situation. There is always some form of selection and filtration.

In terms of digital interactive environments, sound effects and ambient sound can be similarly applied whether it is a wholly virtual experience or representative of an offline product or experience. As mentioned previously, just as music can help depict a company culture, sound effects and ambient sound can portray the 'buzz' of the company. Websites for nightclubs, restaurants, cafes and bars can also benefit from this kind of emotional tagging, and while a website may not allow the user to taste the food or smell the coffee, it may provide some sonic and visual indication of the ambience, how busy and patronized the establishment is, or what a patron might expect. Sound design may even be able to evoke taste and smell synaesthetically. Maintaining consistency and meeting expectations is crucial to the user continuing to suspend their disbelief and sacrifice their time (whether willingly or impulsively) to partake in the world you have constructed for them.

It may be that the minimal expectation of sound on the part of users is the reason behind the general neglect of sound by digital experience designers. However, transcending expectations can also be the source of innovation. For example, Norman (2004: 53) describes a project that introduces sound to photography as a way of enhancing the experience of taking and looking at photos. HP labs in Bristol have been developing 'audiophotographic' photos that combine an audio track which captures:

- Ambient sounds recorded the moment the image is taken, assisting in recall of the event
- Music evoking memories of the event
- Spoken word, allowing interpretation or narration of the event.

Of all the components of sound that can be designed, **dialogue** or the spoken word is probably the least expected by online users. While it is often the major sound consideration in films, what relevance does it have to the online experience? Film dialogue is the product of a script that has undergone numerous iterations. The script editor must decide how to refine and condense the dialogue to within the movie length limit of approximately 120 minutes by dispensing with anything unnecessary to progressing the story efficiently. In the early days of multimedia design, following a film production model, there was reference to scripts to detail the content of CD-ROMs, with scriptwriters contracted to develop these (England and Finney 1999: 120–23). Interestingly, the legacy of this film production model meant that there was also more attention to sound design in the development of multimedia CD-ROMs and this has been inherited and extended by the games industry. But as digital media production became more web-centric, the methodologies evolved and scripts became content inventories. In web development, what were traditionally constituent elements of a script (story, visuals and sound) fall under the umbrella of 'content' and largely refers to text. Thus, the content of a website can be equated with dialogue in film in that it has to be carefully crafted to tell a particular story or convey specific messages. In film, dialogue is literally between characters. In the online domain, dialogue could be conceived of as the conversation an organization wants to have with their customers, and the same questions asked by film script editors apply: what is the story (or message) that needs to be told? Is this content necessary to the story or message? How long is the user expected to engage with the content? Is the content engaging enough to hold the user for the expected amount of time? This sort of dialogue between company and customer does not necessarily have to involve sound. However, one example includes interactive phone systems which are already commonly used. While there is less evidence of this kind of oral/ aural real-time interaction with synthetic agents online, perhaps it will become more widespread with the introduction of voice-command interface technology such as Fonix Speech VoiceIn (http://www.fonixspeech.com). By defining the parameters of verbal interaction, one could be said to be 'writing the dialogue script', providing flexibility in response to user demands and allowing a connection to the audience on a level where emotional performance becomes an active ingredient.

On a more literal level, dialogue as spoken word also has possibilities that have not been thoroughly explored in the online environment. Arguments for improving the accessibility of websites have included providing an audio alternative to screen-based text for people with visual impairment (see the World Wide Web Consortium's Web Content Accessibility Guidelines). As many visually impaired internet users have screen readers which can then be output to speech synthesizers, this means that web content should be designed not only for how it *reads* but also for how it *sounds*.

Summary

After a century of trial-and-error in film sound-production processes, the interactive media industry can now cherry-pick the best of what the last 100 years of cinematic sound design practice has to offer and apply these techniques to the digital environment. Although sound design mechanisms in film have become nuanced and specialized, their capacity to compel the viewer/listener through aural seduction presents potentially powerful lessons for digital designers, in spite of the constraints of experiencing sound on a computer screen compared with the cinematic silver screen. Sound effectively draws users into its world as 'we have eyelids but not earlids' (Welsch cited in Cranny-Francis 2005: 71): that is, we can block out the visual merely by closing our eyes, but it is much more difficult to escape the aural.

As we have detailed above, sound design is a form of emotional design. That is, it uses the design of sonic elements to elicit mood and emotions *from* its audience, or it represents those moods and emotions *to* its audience. The four functions of cinematic sound design that can be leveraged for digital experience design are:

1. Emotional truth

- Pre-conscious processing of sound creates mood, and mood is the filter through which all visual information passes.
- Sound provides the key as to how the visuals are to be received and interpreted by the audience.
- Sound emotionally encodes the content for meaning.

2. Point-of-audition/Point-of-view

- Sound steers an audience's attention through visual information, promoting what is important and in which order, simulating perception and emotional labelling.
- Sound reflects a point-of-view.

3. Storytelling

- Sound connects visual elements to create cinematic phrases, sentences, paragraphs, and ascribes meaning to each.
- Sound 'completes' the visual image by creating a verisimilitude, thus aiding the audience to suspend their disbelief.

4. Physical experience

■ As a result of cross-modal interaction, sound modifies the perception of weight, texture and speed of on-screen objects, lending the visual elements legitimacy as a truthful version of a concrete world (which has important application in 3D virtual-reality environments).

■ Hearing is a form of touch as it has a synaesthetic quality.

■ Sound can maintain the energy level of a sequence even if the visual elements seem 'slow' or 'empty'.

■ An immersive soundfield provides the basis for the visceral experience of spectacle, and the sublime experience of wonder.

References and *recommended reading

Abel, R. and Altman, R. (2001), *The Sounds of Early Cinema*. Bloomington: Indiana University Press.

Bull, M. (2000), *Sounding Out the City: Personal Stereos and the Management of Everyday Life*. New York: Berg.

Chion, M. (1994), *Audio-Vision: Sound on Screen*. New York: Columbia University Press.

*Cranny-Francis, A. (2005), 'Chapter 4 – Sound', in *Multimedia*. London: Sage Publications.

Cubitt, S. (1998), *Digital Aesthetics*. London: Sage.

England, E. and Finney, A. (1999), *Managing Multimedia: Project Management for Interactive Media*. Harlow: Addison-Wesley.

Fonix Speech *VoiceIn* [Online] Available: http://www.fonixspeech.com/index.php. Accessed August 6 2008.

Gaver, W. (1986), 'Auditory icons: Using sound in computer interfaces', Human-Computer Interaction: Journal of Theoretical, Empirical, and Methodological Issues of User Science and of System Design, 2: 2, pp. 167–77.

Holman, T. (1997), *Sound for Film and Television*. Boston: Focal Press.

LeDoux, J. (1998), *The Emotional Brain: the Mysterious Underpinnings of Emotional Life*. New York: Touchstone.

Macaulay, C., Benyon, D. and Crerar, A. (2000), 'Voices in the forest: Sounds, soundscapes and interface design', *Towards a Framework for Design and Evaluation of Navigation in Electronic Spaces*, [Online] Available: http://www.sics.se/humle/projects/persona/web/littsurvey/ch10.pdf. Accessed August 6 2008.

Norman, D. (2004), *Emotional Design: Why we Love (or Hate) Everyday Things*. New York: Basic Books.

Sekular, R., Sekular, A. and Lau, R. (1997) 'Sound alters visual motion perception, *Nature*, 385, p. 308.

Smith, G. (1999), 'Local Emotions, Global Moods' in Plantinga,C. and Smith,G. (eds) *Passionate Views: Film, Cognition and Emotion*. Baltimore: John Hopkins University Press.

Storms, R. (1998) 'Auditory-Visual Cross-Modal Perception Phenomena', United States Navy, Naval PostGraduate School doctoral dissertation, [Online] Available: http://gamepipe.usc.edu/~zyda/Theses/Russell.Storms.PhD.pdf. Accessed July 3 2008.

Tan, E. (1996), *Emotion and the Structure of Narrative Film: Film as an Emotion Machine*. Mahwah: Erlbaum.

Vroomen, J. and de Gelder, B. (2000) 'Sound enhances visual perception: cross-modal effects of auditory organization on vision', *Journal of Experimental Psychology: Human Perception and Performance*, 26: 5, pp. 1583–1590.

Vroomen, J. and de Gelder, B. (2004) 'Temporal Ventriloquism: Sound Modulates the Flash-Lag Effect', *Journal of Experimental Psychology: Human Perception and Performance*, 30: 3, pp. 513–518.

World Wide Web Consortium (2004) 'Web Content Accessibility Guidelines' [Online] Available: http://www.w3.org/TR/WCAG20. Accessed August 6 2008.

Architectures of the Physical and Virtual: Parallel Design Principles in Built and Digital Environments

Linda Leung and Meaghan Waters

What are the similarities between information/experience architecture and built architecture? How do their practices intersect? There are parallels and divergences in the training given to architects and digital experience designers which impacts the ways design is approached and incorporated into the development process. Architecture students are taught to approach design with both an overall vision in mind and a consideration and respect for the materials to be used and how these will influence the final design – in other words, both top-down and bottom-up design work off each other iteratively. This has both similarities and differences with digital experience design in terms of the tensions between (top-down) user-centred interaction design processes and (bottom-up) software engineering methodologies. In architecture, there is training in how space and people interact with each other and how all the design disciplines involved in a build must cooperate with each other. However, the consideration of space and the harnessing of other disciplines in digital experience design is yet to reach its full potential.

Top-down and bottom-up

Meaghan initially decided to be an architect because she was interested in the way that people use buildings. It was people's relationships to buildings that enticed her into the profession, not the desire to just make something on a large scale. This also applies to her work in digital environments: it is not creation for the sake of creation; rather, understanding the relationship between user and application is fundamental to developing something that works at a functional as well as experiential level.

The crux of her architectural training was learning to negotiate these two dimensions of design. Architects must have a 'vision' for a building, yet acknowledge that this will be affected by the materials used. The tiles, bricks, etc. used in a building are determined by the overall vision of the architect. Simultaneously, this vision can be realized or compromised by those very materials. The experience and accessibility of a building is made or broken by the materials that constitute it.

In relation to web design, this means that a digital experience is informed by how a site is developed. There are certain considerations that are non-negotiable. Just as fire alarms in buildings are mandatory, there are aspects of online safety (such as secure socket layers in e-commerce) that are absolutely necessary to protect users. Similarly, designing a website to be accessible by means other than a mouse and keyboard should be assumed as in designing a building for different kinds of access: for example, beyond just wheelchair access, there are people with prams or shopping trolleys; emergency exits (when lifts or escalators fail) and entrances (for ambulance crews and fire officers); trucks which need to deliver or remove goods; hallways and corridors that need to be amenable to furniture being transported between floors. How do you get power in and waste out of a building, just as you have data inputs and outputs from a website? These issues have to be integrated into the design process, not take the form of add-ons after a building or website has been developed. As web design becomes a respected profession, it is becoming increasingly evident that expertise is necessary in establishing and managing a website, in the same way that almost all building design and construction requires the input of an architect.

Meaghan describes the architect's vision as a 'top-down' approach to design. Particular architectural movements are underpinned by ideological and philosophical trends in what and how buildings should be (see Kohler 2007 and Colquhoun 2002). For instance, classical pre-modern styles of architecture aimed for 'formal and elaborate beauty'; in contrast to Bauhaus which was oriented towards the future rather than the past, embracing the latest technologies and materials to produce buildings which were 'simple and unpretentious' (Bush-Brown 1976: 39). Buildings that are 'vision-led' are distinctive in their design and often articulate the unique style and 'signature' of the chief architect through both form and technology (the materials used and the way it is built). Examples of visionary buildings include Jorn Utzon's Sydney Opera House, and Frank Gehry's Guggenheim Museum in Bilbao, Spain (see Artifice Inc 2007).

However, there are scarce examples of digital experiences that have a signature design (an exception being Pixar films, stories and animation). While there are many websites that share the same style or look, few are uniquely identifiable as the product of a particular individual or team. Perhaps this is because there is no role within a web development team that is particularly senior, and it is these egalitarian relationships within a web team that make it more difficult to move beyond mere agreement about the 'look and feel' of a site (or just *form* in architectural terms) to a collective vision of its experience and utility, or in other words, a marriage of *form* and *function* as seen in the 'close conceptual relationship between aesthetics and technology' of successful architectural projects (Risebero 1992: 127). These higher aims can also be lost in the struggle to balance client demands with user requirements to the extent that the aim of creating an overarching experience becomes compromised.

If web development teams were organized similarly to teams working in built architecture, the role of the experience designer on a web project could be appropriately likened to that of a chief architect on a building project. Based on their market and user research, their responsibility is to develop a vision for the client but aimed at the user, convince the client as well as the project team of its importance, and ensure that it is implemented. The individual vision of a chief architect on a building project is arguably intellectually, conceptually, historically and practically driven. To be visionary requires knowledge of and reference to design theory, history and practices. Good architects draw upon this disciplinary baggage. But can an experience architect on a web project be expected to do the same given the shorter history, dearth of theory and fewer standards in online design?

The hierarchy within a building project allows the chief architect to exercise similar responsibilities to that of an experience designer, back-end developer and visual designer on a web project. In other words, the architect ultimately directs the user experience of the building as well as how it looks, and the materials which form it. But it is the role of the team working under him/her to work out the best possible process by which to realize this vision and then implement it. It is at this point where the top-down approach (the vision that has come from the top) has to be reconciled from the bottom-up (in the detail and procedures which allow the building to be built as well as function as it should).

The risk of having a predominantly top-down approach is that the integrity of the vision is maintained while everything else can get compromised as it drives down into the detail. This can be seen in buildings that have a gorgeous facade but do not actually work well on the inside. The Sydney Opera House is an internationally recognized icon that successfully brands Australia. However, as an opera house, it does not seat the numbers originally intended and is not large enough to stage full-scale operas; the orchestra pit has been reported as too cramped for the musicians; and the high roof has resulted in problems with the acoustics. The inside does not live up to the outside, in part, because it was not faithful to the original vision of chief architect, Jorn Utzon. It was so compromised by budget cuts and political interference that Utzon resigned mid-project and his designs were subsequently altered (see Watson 2006).

This prioritization of style over substance is a familiar one in online design, when the 'bells and whistles' overpower the utility and purpose of a website. Even in cases where the experience architect has developed a clear vision and strategy on a project, this is not always respected by other members of the web team, particularly when there is a lack of coordination in the bottom up approach. As Meaghan says: '...architecture does train you for the disappointments that interaction design also gives to you. You design something and then someone else comes along and builds it. To some extent, they get the last say...'

A bottom-up approach entails integrating all the components in a way that will work. If it is done well, it should still be consistent with the vision. However, when working at a micro-level upwards, preoccupation with detail can mean the vision can be lost. For example, the garden shed that is built to accommodate the lawn mower and gardening tools may be fine for that purpose, but it may be in the wrong place in the garden if it is unintentionally visible from the street. Likewise, Meaghan contends that much software design is done this way: cobbling together functionality in an interface before thinking about how this will be used in everyday work practices and its effects on workflow as well as work culture. Web-based applications internal to organizations, such as customer or employee databases, often illustrate the dangers of a bottom-up approach in the absence of a high-level vision.

> it's basically anything where you can't easily move from one piece of it to another piece in a common task that has been designed from a bottom up approach with no one actually looking at the overall view on it...anything where you get a lot of pop up windows coming up, one after the other after the other, is a great example of no one ever having thought about how it's all going to hold together.

On the more positive side, Facebook exemplifies an application that has numerous component parts that are held together by a broad vision and purpose of social networking. LinkedIn operates similarly on a functional level, but has a different vision and purpose of professional networking.

From architect to seamstress
After studying architecture during an economic recession, Meaghan found opportunities for employment in the field limited. She therefore fell back on her dressmaking skills to supplement her income, designing and making wedding gowns. Although the transition from architecture to dressmaking may not seem a logical one, the relationship between buildings and the body is not a new one. Historically, buildings based on the body can be found as far back as the Renaissance and are articulated in more contemporary ways with notions of bodies as temples and cosmetic surgery as a form of architecting bodies (Jones 2007: 186). Thus, in dressmaking, Meaghan was still able to apply architectural principles of balancing top-down and bottom-up approaches to design and construction.

Firstly, her clients each had a vision for their wedding dress, having been unable to find what they wanted from retailers. But the dressmaker has to be clear about what the client envisages: 'Everyone has a vision of what they want to look like on their wedding day, and it was my job to tease out that vision, convey it back to the person who's going to wear it and then make it happen in a way that matches to the vision.'

Next, the dressmaker has to work out how the gown is to be constructed while still ensuring it can be worn practically: 'It's got to be built in something and it's got to fit the person that's wearing it. They've got to be able to walk in it and they've got to be able to do all these things in it.'

Dressmaking could be described as small-scale architecture in that you are designing for one person and one day. But the negotiation between the top-down and bottom-up approaches remain the same: the bride has to feel fabulous as well as be able to breathe, walk and eat in her dress. A wedding dress has an emotional impact that long outlives its utilitarian value. How the bride felt wearing the gown, how the fabric felt against her skin will forever be associated with memories of her wedding day.

Like built architecture, dressmaking involves the design of space – the space around the body, how one moves and functions in that space, and the emotions that are attached to that space. These spatial-affective elements are well understood in architecture and dressmaking, but the role of space in emotional design has not been fully explored in digital experiences. While there has been research on the emotional responses of users in 3D virtual environments (see Li, Daugherty and Biocca 2003), web interactions are still primarily two-dimensional. There is still much to be understood about the emotional design of everyday online transactions: '... what you design has an emotional impact and the space has a feel to it...you could walk into a room completely with your eyes shut and you can get a feeling for the space in it because of the way the air feels and the ambient sounds within it.'

How an object and/or/in space (whether building, wedding gown or web application) can be built for use as well as desirability is the concern of the architect, dressmaker and experience designer. Indeed, any kind of design field and training requires an understanding that an object's use goes beyond just pure utility: people also have to want to use it and the designer's role is to evoke that desire. 'I got into architecture initially because I just wanted to build things and make people feel good...Online design is also about looking great and feeling great to use...People generally want to feel good and you want to build things that make people feel good, whatever it is.'

Architectural training
Meaghan's training as an architect concentrated on four core areas: design, theory, history and practice. Students were exposed to ideas and philosophies of architecture, as well as architectural trends and movements over time. This fed into their own approaches and attempts to design before working in collaboration with other design students to implement their proposals. Within these core areas, subjects were shared with students of landscape design and building services design, so that when it came to practice, the teams mimicked those in which they would be working as future qualified architects in industry (Geddes 2006: 57).

Although having architecture students do the same subjects as students from other design fields is indicative of the multi-disciplinary nature of design, it is also evidence of the commonalities between what Meaghan calls the 'hard' design disciplines. These are fields of design which involve the production of an object that will be subject to physical interaction: that is, it will be either picked up, walked through, thrown, or pressed, etc. These design disciplines include not only architecture and related fields such as landscape design, building services design and interior design; but also industrial design, product design, ergonomics and human-computer interaction: '...what they're trained to do is understand that people are, in fact, actually going to interact with this. They are going to touch it, to feel it, to move around with it, to do something in it and to directly engage with it, physically engage with it.'

It is this sort of training that was missing in the early days of online design, resulting in the kind of websites produced by graphic design bureaus that simply attempted to transfer print design principles to the web, and which subsequently ignited the usability movement. These had all the information required, but did not address the issue of how it was to be accessed and used.

During Meaghan's architecture training, she was discouraged from taking briefs (for example, from clients wanting to build a family home) in terms of simply asking what kind of rooms they wanted in the house (such as three bedrooms with an eat-in kitchen, etc). Rather than just figuring out the component parts, it was necessary to ascertain how the family would use the house. (Would the children share a bedroom? Would the study be used by everyone? Does the family eat together at mealtimes? What does each family member need and want in the new home? What were their expectations of the new home?) There are many ways a three-bedroom home can be designed. Two homes may have the same facilities (number of bedrooms, laundry, kitchen, living room, etc.) but present and feel very differently.

Again, these approaches are beginning to be used online, now that products (such as Facebook and LinkedIn) which are functionally equivalent have to differentiate themselves through the experiences and vision they bring to their users.

Summary

- Hierarchy is not inherently bad: in built architecture, it enables an architect's vision to shine through and thus can facilitate innovation.
- A top-down approach is where a creative vision determines the design.
- A bottom-up approach involves the practical means of realizing the vision.
- A successful design negotiates the top-down vision from the bottom up.
- It takes a huge amount of effort, confidence and conviction to push a vision through.
- That spatial and tactile design has an emotional impact is well understood in architecture, dressmaking and other 'hard' design disciplines, but has not been fully exploited in 'soft' digital and virtual environments, especially in web design.
- Digital experience design must go beyond gathering functional requirements, but also understand how functions are performed and applications used in the context of users' lives.

References and *recommended reading

Artifice Inc. (2007), 'Great buildings online' [Online] Available: http://www.greatbuildings.com. Accessed August 15 2008.

Bush-Brown, H. (1976), *Beaux Arts to Bauhaus and Beyond*. New York: Whitney Library of Design.

Colquhoun, A. (2002), *Modern Architecture*. Oxford: Oxford University Press.

Geddes, R. (2006), 'Second thoughts: Reflections on winning second prize', in A. Watson (ed.), *Building a Masterpiece: The Sydney Opera House*. Sydney: Powerhouse Publishing.

Jones, M. (2007) *Skintight: An Anatomy of Cosmetic Surgery*. Oxford: Berg.

Kohler, C. (2007), 'A brief history of architectural styles and movements', *Associated Content* [Online] Available: http://www.associatedcontent.com/article/230545/a_brief_history_of_architectural_ styles.html. Accessed 8 May 2007.

*Li, H., Daugherty, T. and Biocca, F. (2003), 'The role of virtual experience in consumer learning', *Journal of Consumer Psychology*, 13: 4, pp. 395–407.

Risebero, B. (1992), *Fantastic Form: Architecture and Planning Today*. London: The Herbert Press.

*Watson, A. (ed.) (2006), *Building a Masterpiece: The Sydney Opera House*. Sydney: Powerhouse Publishing.

10

ART AND ARTICULATION: THE FINER POINTS OF ENGAGING THE USER IN ABSTRACT CONCEPTS AND LATERAL THINKING

Linda Leung and Scott Bryant

Fine art challenges its audience to engage with abstract concepts that may not be easily articulated and require introspective reflection. The art gallery offers a rich metaphor for conceptualizing digital experiences: just as the gallery is the space where the spectator engages with works of art, digital worlds represent the interface between users and content. Furthermore, the art world creates experiences that enable users to tackle challenging content, and elevates content to the level of the sacred. This can be applied in digital design to contexts where complex ideas take primacy. However, conceptualizing an online environment as a gallery and its content as 'art' can mean contravening web usability principles which assume task-oriented, utilitarian and time-constrained online interactions.

This chapter examines the ways in which art is presented, and the design of experiences of art. The instruments which 'frame' an artwork and scaffold the experience for the spectator are discussed in relation to how such techniques can be translated for digital contexts.

Scott explores the differences and similarities between art and design, in terms of his training as an artist, and his work as an experience architect. How does his development process as an artist intersect or diverge from what he does as a designer?

The gallery as interface
Going to see an exhibition is more than just about experiencing art. It is a highly designed experience which is framed in a way to set up and fulfill certain expectations before the spectator even enters the exhibition space.

When visiting an art gallery, one anticipates the art work to take 'centre stage'. The works of art are intended to take precedence over the space or architecture in which they are presented. In more simplistic terms, it could be said that the art and what it conveys is the point of focus and prioritized over the gallery or exhibition space. In the art world, galleries are often referred to as 'white cubes': that is, they are designated as neutral spaces which are supposed to be visually, sensorially and experientially unobtrusive. They are 'blank canvases' that recede into the background when they are filled with art. 'Fundamentally, exhibition-making is focused on the content of the works to be displayed and concerns the ordering of these works as a sequence, to be understood in relation to each other and in dialogue with the conditions of the viewing environment.' (Dernie 2006: 6)

A corporate website can be similarly conceptualized as a 'blank canvas' or neutral space in which an individual or organization presents their 'message' or content. Applying this metaphor means the architecture of the site and the presentation of the content should not distract from the content itself. This approach is also illustrated in Nielsen's usability guidelines (2000), which advocate aesthetic and minimalist presentation and toning down distinctive design. Content is king, while the shell in which the content sits ought to take a back seat.

The problem with the notion of 'content' is that it suggests material that is not particularly meaningful. Instead, perhaps digital experience designers should regard content as having the status or importance of works of art. In this way, only content that has been carefully crafted is made public. A shared digital environment (including intranet or public website) should not be seen as simply a storage mechanism for any old content. Rather, it is an exhibition space for work which has undergone a thorough development process and which is worthy of showing to users. Furthermore, 'content' implies a critical mass or volume of material, whereas art is about delivering key messages through an object or work. Elevating content to the level of art means applying the old adage 'less is more' and doing more with less.

Artists and art critics discuss art works in terms of their 'conceptual rigour'. That is, an art work is judged according to the relationship between what the work is trying to convey (its 'key message'), its medium (the materials used), its form (its characteristics, scale, size, construction, architecture) and presentation (the manner in which it is shown). To what extent is the relationship between these aspects resolved and coherent? '...an exhibition design considers the simple dialogue between the objects to be exhibited and the space in which they are presented: where the objects are, and how they are arranged will determine the nature of the message they communicate.' (Dernie 2006: 6)

A glance at many organizational websites would indicate that such 'conceptual rigour' is missing. For example, a corporate website which functions as a dumping ground for every piece of content produced by the organization can be inconsistent with the 'key message' of its branding if the company markets its knowledge as exclusive and desirable. As an exhibition space for the organization, the website conveys to the user a confusing array of messages which they must decode in order to work out which are important. Conceptually, there is a lack of resolution between what the organization seeks to say about itself, and how it does this through its online presence. Thus, the website could not really be considered a great work of art.

An exception to the rule of 'content is king' is the Guggenheim Museum, in both its online and offline manifestations. The physical architecture of the New York museum could be seen as overpowering or competing with the artworks that it exhibits. However, the distinctiveness and innovation of its architecture has come to be associated with the kind of art that is shown there. In this regard, both the art and architecture are equally reputable and complementary. In its online capacity, the Guggenheim Virtual Museum (http://www.guggenheim.org/exhibitions/virtual/virtual_museum.html) demonstrates a consistency in its experimentation with virtual space to allow users to experience its art collections. The Guggenheim brand is exceptional in its ability to achieve this coherence in its 'message' across media, particularly in a digital arena that inherently devalues content due its ready availability.

While many websites have gallery sections, this chapter argues that a website (and indeed any openly available digital offering) in its entirety can be regarded as a gallery, a space which presents the work of an individual or organization to a public. This opens up opportunities to think beyond the 'page paradigm' of websites, and instead consider a company's online presence as an extension of how it presents itself in other ways to the world: whether it is its headquarters, offices, staff, CEO, employee uniforms, all these artefacts are means of exhibiting the company to others. Therefore, the work that is presented online should be accorded the status of 'art' by the digital designer as well as the spectator in that it ideally would have been subject to much reflection and revision before being exhibited.

Art criticism and interpretation
To fully appreciate a work of art takes time. A gallery invites the spectator to quietly ponder the meaning of the work. One is not expected to understand it immediately because its meaning is often complex and open to interpretation. Therefore, the spectator is free to linger and muse upon the artwork. To apply this to the online world runs counter to usability principles which assert that websites must have 'zero learning time or die' (Nielsen 2000). Going to an art gallery is not meant to be a hurried or pressing experience. Nor is it intended to be task-driven so that the spectator leaves as soon as they have looked at the work and 'get it'. For example, the Porsche website (http://www.porsche.com) allows the user to find the specifications for a specific model, but still manages to convey their cars and the site itself as works of art, inviting the user to appreciate the quality and detail of each.

If websites can be thought of as gallery spaces, then users should also feel welcome and enticed to consider the content in their own time and at their own pace. This necessitates content that is worthy of the user's time and which engages them in a way which is both intellectually and sensorially stimulating. The 'key message/s' that are to be conveyed do not have to be simple, but they do have to encourage the user to think. This is harder than it sounds. It is far more difficult for an organization to depict its values, principles or ethics through its online presence in a profound and memorable way, than to just include a superficial statement in the 'About

Us' section of the company website which is concerned mainly with helping users find information in the quickest possible way. To be able to draw in users through abstract concepts is critical to any organization that trades on its ideas. Just as art can get spectators to confront heavyweight issues, users can be willing to tackle complex subjects – such as inequality, identity, stereotypes, compassion in an age of excess – if given appropriate contexts to do so. However, the experience has to be designed to be conducive to this sort of contemplation.

In a gallery, the spectator is provided with clues, as well as tools or instruments to assist them in their interpretation of an artwork. The gallery environment clearly differentiates between what is art and what is not. It is evident what the spectator should be looking at. The artwork might be framed and mounted on the wall (if it is a painting), or placed on a plinth covered with a glass box (if it is a sculpture). In an online context, this equates to flagging important content, presenting it in a way which highlights that which is important and that which is not. Furthermore, an exhibition generally provides a room sheet, catalogue essay or audio guide for the spectator to either introduce them to the work or aid them in interpreting it. These tell the spectator where the work is located, what it is made from and offer a perspective of what the work is about. This can be applied in an online environment as a kind of scaffolding which helps orient the user and provides an entry to content which may be quite challenging.

The history of modern art provides an insight into experimentations with traditional forms of representation. Where pre-modern painting was traditionally a means of recording history through portraits, landscapes and 'still life'; modern art pioneered visual styles (such as Impressionism, Cubism, Surrealism, etc.) that depicted the world in different ways. It changed the purpose as well as the user experience of art from merely being an historical archive to challenging people's perceptions of the world. Online design is arguably still in its pre-modern era, given that many websites function as digital repositories, rather than aim for loftier objectives such as offering an alternative vision.

Perhaps online ventures such as Second Life have succeeded because they enable a change in perspective. It provides a contemplative space similar to that of a gallery through which the user can experience the world in a different way. It is an unhurried environment that allows the user to interact with others and things beyond what might be deemed 'normal' in the offline world. It epitomizes many of values of Surrealism, Pop and Conceptual Art movements in that the user can be confronted by the downright bizarre, while simultaneously closely referencing the social context of 'real life'. Like much great art, it asks, tests and questions who we are.

The phenomenon of Second Life also reflects the trend in contemporary art of letting the audience determine the outcome of an artwork: '...exhibition design now tends to be explicitly audience-focused' (Dernie 2006: 13).

The art world calls this relational aesthetics, whereby the experience of an artwork is shaped by the people who interact with or participate in it. Bourriaud (2002) calls this 'interactive' art because it concerns human-to-human encounters; it experiments with sociality and ways of bringing people together whereby the artwork becomes an arena of exchange. For example, artist Lincoln Tobier set up a radio station in galleries and invited the public to discuss their views which were then broadcast over the airwaves (ibid.: 32). Felix Gonzalez-Torres' work, 'Stacks', is a pile of sweets from which the visitor is welcome to pick; however, the visitor is faced with the responsibility of diminishing the work by taking away from it (ibid.: 39). Gabriel Orozco slings a hammock in the garden of the Museum of Modern Art in New York, with no restrictions on how visitors use it (ibid.: 17). Hurst (2007) calls artist Richard Serra 'a great American experience designer' whose 'explicit focus [is] on creating an *experience*, rather than an object to be revered...Here's the old way: a painting hangs on a gallery wall, and we, the subject, are invited to look at it, the object. We're here, and it's there. In contrast, Serra's work makes *us* the object. As you walk through the mazelike structure of "Sequence", for example, the art's impact is on your own personal experience walking through the space...The steel just sets up the context for the experience (always note the importance of setting context when creating good experience!)'.

Again, the online world has mirrored these orchestrations in human contact, immediacy and proximity through Web 2.0 and the growth of user-generated content. This can be deemed a form of relational aesthetics, as it is essentially about the relationship between the user, the content and other users. In the art of relational aesthetics, the dynamic between the spectator, the work and other spectators is explored by requiring the spectator to become an active participant in the work. The distance that usually exists between the artist and the passive viewer is contested as elitist. The perception of art as the product of the sole creative effort of an artist is also challenged. The artist relinquishes control over the creative process and submits it to the collaborative process. The kind of art that is produced is aesthetically different and not always pleasing to the eye, giving primacy to the social over the visual.

Relational aesthetics may result in an art product that is not aesthetically pleasing (for example, huge amounts of user-generated content). In terms of online relational aesthetics, this is exemplified in MySpace, which has become known for its 'ugliness', although part of its appeal lies in the ability of the user to 'beautify' or make their mark on it (Porter 2006). It, too, priorities social design over visual design: it provides a social framework in which users can engage in creative collaboration. Perhaps its popularity can be attributed to the opportunities it offers to users to partake in artistic practice. Relational aesthetics may even be deployed in an organizational website which acts as a content 'dumpster'. It is the participatory process of a website which relies on user contributions that makes it artistic and distinguishes it from the content-rich corporate website which does not. Art is no longer about the visual: it is determined by process rather than outcome. The traditional question of 'what is art?' becomes superceded by the question of '*when* is art?' (Ardenne et al. 1999: 40, my emphasis).

Contemporary art practice as seen in relational aesthetics, other movements such as Conceptual Art, and forms of installation challenge traditional economies of exchange. The economic value of a work of art is called into question, as it cannot be purchased like a painting and hung on the wall of the buyer's home. Indeed, as art objects are not functional, the worth of an artwork is always open to debate. Similarly, popular and successful online phenomena such as YouTube, MySpace, Flickr and Second Life all disrupt conventional business models. Like expensive works of art, they are worth large sums of money despite being unable to explicitly demonstrate their financial value.

The artistic process

Artists, whether formally educated or not, enter their professional practice knowing that their work is valued, appreciated and even judged according to sets of culturally determined criteria. In isolation, the criteria are quite abstract in relation to the way the art is appreciated as a whole. For example, a work of art can be appreciated purely for its use of 'line' or 'form' while the content or the meaning of the artwork operates on another level of appreciation. Conversely, the use of 'line' and 'form' could be the elements that enable our understanding or experience of that content on an emotional level. Whether considered separately or in combination, it could be argued that these criteria form a platform for the experience of art itself. These sets of criteria not only influence the way artists work and create art but also the way in which art is positioned and understood. Artists when creating art are conscious of this 'language' of appreciation criteria and once their work is exhibited, they know their art will be discussed in relation to those criteria. This language has been built upon over time often in response to trends in art and culture.

These criteria for art appreciation include:

- **Form**, the physical qualities of the work shaped by the materials it uses. Beaird (2007) recommends visual design should aim to please users through its form, but how can we think about form digitally? Perhaps it is more difficult to think about websites in terms of form because they are 'soft' and largely two-dimensional, whereas in art, form refers to an object's three-dimensionality, its weight, the way it feels to touch or hold it. Art innovation comes from experimentations in form, and so it is important to learn how to articulate and manipulate form digitally as well.
- **Content**, the artwork's subject matter, what it is or represents, and the emotions, ideas, symbols, narratives, or spiritual connotations it suggests. In the digital arena, content is understood well as the ultimate drawcard for users (Beaird 2007). Content is king in design circles, but as in art, the key concepts and ideas are more difficult to convey well.
- **Feeling**, the emotional design and impact of a work. Art can achieve this affect through the simplest of design elements: it may be through a colour combination or contrast that a particular feeling is evoked. Online design is still in its early days of learning the importance of engaging emotion in the user experience.
- **Critical opinion**, the public response to a work of art or an exhibition of work. There are different spheres in which this takes place in the art world: in the media (in newspapers and magazines reviewing art) and in education (in institutions where teaching and learning of art takes place). This critique of art across different arenas operates as a kind of quality assurance, pushing the artist to strive for critical acclaim. The digital world needs a similar level of critical discourse in order to encourage innovation and extend the boundaries of design.

- **Craftsmanship**, or the quality of the technical execution of the work. In the work of a professional artist, the craftsmanship is clearly more sophisticated than that of an amateur. Likewise, the technical execution of a website says as much about the coder/programmer as it does about what it represents. In some cases, a website that appears to be the work of a single person might imply a lack of professionalism and/or a budget paucity. Web craftsmanship can also refer to the ability to adapt a website for the end-user experience, such as dial-up or broadband, or making CSS and slick Javascript work across different browser versions.
- **Art history**, the diversity of movements which artists reference and extend in their work. This is rich tradition into which other design disciplines tap, as online design should too. Design has inherited much from the world of art, and digital experience design needs to exploit that heritage to elevate the discipline to an art form.

Print media, graphic design, architecture, photography and cinema have also adopted much of this language of art appreciation. Designers are arguably practicing as artists on many levels, but added to their discipline is the requirement to create for function and use. Therefore, it is also necessary for them to be educated in and familiar with the levels of art appreciation. Indeed, many of the principles of design historically come from art. 'In the Renaissance there was no clear distinction between branches of the arts. For example, such artists as Michelangelo and Raphael were called upon to practice all three of the major fine arts.' (Bush-Brown 1976: 91)

These major fine arts included painting, sculpture and architecture. In other words, artists were also design practitioners. 'The artists of the Renaissance used divine proportion to design their paintings, sculpture and architecture just as designers today often employ this ratio when creating page layouts, posters and brochures.' (Beaird 2007)

Likewise, interactive media and particularly the web as an emerging popular medium of our time is increasingly being subject to a specific language of appreciation that incorporates and builds upon the language of art appreciation. Websites are quite often judged appreciated and experienced on what Garrett (2003: 140–59) describes as the 'surface plane' of visual design according to his 'elements of user experience'. These judgements in relation to visual design and the 'surface plane' have been found in research studies (Skatssoon, 2006) to be crucial to whether a user will stay on a website. Remarkably 'visual appeal can be assessed within 50 milliseconds, suggesting that web designers have about 50 milliseconds to make a good impression'. This does suggest that in terms of websites that the 'medium is the message' and as in art, the visual design is very much part of how we make sense of content.

The high level of visual literacy of users means that, at the very least, online designers must understand the basic elements and principles of design. The elements of design are the fundamental 'building blocks' of design, and are not only used in art, but in visual design, architecture and other design disciplines. According to McClurg-Genevese (2005a), Zelanski and Fisher (1988), they include:

- line
- shape and form
- texture (the suggestion of form through for example, the bevelled edges of a button which give the impression that it can be pressed)
- value and weight (contrast and salience)
- colour (the vocabulary of colour, emotional effects of colour, warm and cool colours, advancing and receding colours, colour combinations, limited and open palette)
- time (the duration of viewing a piece of work).

It is not the intention of this chapter to elaborate on these elements of design, as any introductory art book will do this better. However, while this is terminology familiar to visual designers, it is also imperative for digital experience designers to understand the role of these elements in the design of human-computer interaction. The element of time is especially relevant because, as mentioned above, the digital experience designer has far less time (50 milliseconds to be precise) in which to impress the user than the artist (whose viewer can ponder the work at their leisure).

The elements themselves do not determine good art or design, but how they are used, combined and applied through the principles of design. The factors which inform how the elements are deployed include:

- variety
- rhythm
- balance (symmetrical and asymmetrical)
- compositional unity (proximity, repetition)
- emphasis through placement, continuance, isolation, contrast, proportion
- economy
- relationship to the environment (context, site specificity).

Beaird (2007) and McClurg-Genevese (2005b) give examples of how these principles are used well in web design. Beaird argues that good design is like a language: just as only certain configurations of words make sense, there are a limited combination of elements and principles of design that work or are aesthetically pleasing.

Aesthetics is now being discussed within the discipline of interaction design (Dimond 2007, Heller 2005 and Lowgren 2006) and so there is a growing acknowledgement that interactive media is experienced and even judged according to a new language of appreciation criteria. This is because the aesthetics of digital experience design are made more complex by the additional ingredient of interaction. That is, it goes far beyond the visual. User interaction means that a website's relationship to its environment can constantly change. Whereas in art, the viewing context might be in a gallery or a site where public art is exhibited; there are a multitude of contexts in which a single website is seen. Firstly, it competes with a deluge of other content in the online environment (compared with the conventional sparseness of art work in a gallery separated by large amounts of space). Secondly, search engines shape and filter the context for a website to be accessed and viewed. Thirdly, the website is seen within the user's environment: on their browser and operating system, probably while they are using other applications, and in any possible physical location.

Thus, the aesthetics of digital design are complicated, but simultaneously, can also be as distinctive as any kind of art movement. For example, early hand-coded HTML websites had their own unique aesthetic that included limited hypertext interaction. These were superceded by more 'designerly' websites, many developed in Flash, which generated a very different aesthetic with newer and more experimental forms of interaction but arguably poor usability. Then came Web 2.0, with its 'ugly' but highly usable relational aesthetics. Now the exploration of three-dimensional spaces online through, for example, Google Earth and Second Life has heralded a new aesthetic age, one of 'pliability'. Pliable interaction is pseudo-tactile, allowing the user to feel the interaction as one more closely aligned to the offline world. The ability to 'zoom in' smoothly and gracefully to a closer view of the Earth from outer space down to a specific neighbourhood is an example of this.

> The notion of pliability is an attempt to articulate a certain quality in using digital, interactive products and services. The use of a digital artifact is characterized as pliable if it feels like a tightly connected loop between eye and hand, between action and response. A pliable interaction is one where the user is drawn into a sense of shaping the digital information with her fingertips, even though the actual artifact might employ standard, non-tactile interaction techniques such as mouse, keyboard and a display monitor. Pliability is a sensuous quality, having to do with how it feels to use the artifact in the here-and-now of the use situation, and as such it plays a role in understanding the aesthetics of interaction. (Lowgren 2006: 3)

New aesthetics emerge with the introduction of new technologies, and exploration of their possibilities as well as their constraints. For example, AJAX has brought another kind of aesthetic to the web, one which provides an alternative to the 'page refresh' when, for example, an online form has not been fully completed. Instead, only the incomplete sections of the form are highlighted. On the other hand, it is still difficult to translate fluorescent colours for online media, and so a digital aesthetic has a limited colour palette compared to the aesthetics of print media. Aesthetics is informed by what you can and can't do with a medium. Thus, digital aesthetics are very much technologically determined and this is where it differs from art.

Art is determined by the artist: the artist is inspired to create their own personal vision and finds the most appropriate materials to realize this. This sort of vision can be translated to the digital arena by organizations and communities. Perhaps thinking about websites as works of art, and subjecting them to the same criteria that art critics employ, would bring greater rigour and innovation to online design, and elevate their status in the design world.

Summary

■ The notion of a website as a gallery forces designers to think about value of the content that is to be exhibited.

■ Thinking about content as 'art' necessitates revision and reflection on the key messages to be conveyed and the way they are to be presented.

■ Environments in which art is exhibited challenge spectators to confront difficult and abstract concepts in their own time: examples of this sort of space online are rare because usability principles recommend designing for ease and efficiency.

■ Online ventures which have followed the footsteps of modern art in providing new perspectives of the world that contest traditional methods and economies of exchange have been popular and successful.

■ Exposing digital design to the same level of review and critique as art would encourage greater innovation and improve rigour in the discipline.

■ Any kind of designer from any kind of design discipline (including digital experience architects and interaction designers) should be familiar with the basic elements and principles of design, even if it is to contradict them. This is not the sole terrain of visual or graphic designers.

References and *recommended reading

Ardenne, P., Beausse, P. and Goumare, L. (1999), *Contemporary Art Practices: Art as Experience*. Paris: Editions Dis Voir.

Beaird, J. (2007), *The Principles of Beautiful Web Design* [Online] Available: http://www.sitepoint.com/print/principles-beautiful-web-design. Accessed August 6 2008.

Bourriaud, N. (2002), *Relational Aesthetics*. France: Les presses du reel.

Bush-Brown, H. (1976), *Beaux Arts to Bauhaus and Beyond*. New York: Whitney Library of Design.

*Dernie, D. (2006), *Exhibition Design*. New York: W.W. Norton & Co.

Dimond, J. (2007), *Aesthetics and Usability: What Can Interface Design Learn from Painting?* [Online] Available: http://www.blinkinteractive.com/ourexperience/essays/2007/01/aesthetics_and_usability_what.php. Accessed January 15 2007.

Garrett, J. (2003), *The Elements of User Experience, User Centered Design for the Web*. New York: New Riders

Heller, D. (2005), 'Aesthetics and interaction design: Some preliminary thoughts', *Interactions*, September–October [Online] Available: http://portal.acm.org/citation.cfm?doid=1082369.1082400. Accessed August 6 2008.

Hurst, M. (2007), 'Richard Serra and experience design', *goodexperience.com* [Online] Available: http://www.goodexperience.com/blog/archives/005664.php. Accessed June 28 2007.

Lowgren, J. (2006), 'Pliability as an experiential quality: Exploring the aesthetics of interaction design', *Artifact*, 1: 2, pp. 85–95, [Online] Available: http://webzone.k3.mah.se/k3jolo/Material/pliabilityFinalPre.pdf. Accessed August 6 2008.

McClurg-Genevese, J. (2005a), 'The elements of design', *Digital Web Magazine* [Online] Available: http://www.digital-web.com/articles/elements_of_design. Accessed August 15 2005.

McClurg-Genevese, J. (2005b), 'The principles of design', *Digital Web Magazine* [Online] Available: http://www.digital-web.com/articles/principles_of_design. Accessed August 15 2005.

Nielsen, J. (2000), 'End of web design' [Online] Available: http://www.useit.com/alertbox/20000723.html. Accessed August 6 2008.

Porter, J. (2006), 'Ugliness, social design, and the MySpace lesson' [Online] Available: http://bokardo.com/archives/do-myspace-users-have-bad-taste. Accessed August 18 2006.

Skatssoon, J. (2006), 'Web users are quick to judge' [Online] Available: http://www.abc.net.au/news/newsitems/200601/s1548520.htm. Accessed January 16 2006.

Zelanski, P. and Fisher, M. (1988), *The Art of Seeing*. Englewood Cliffs: Prentice-Hall.

BIBLIOGRAPHY

Abel, R. and Altman, R. (2001), *The Sounds of Early Cinema*. Bloomington: Indiana University Press.

Agins, T. (1999), *The End of Fashion: How Marketing Changed the Clothing Business Forever*. New York: Quill.

Ardenne, P., Beausse, P. and Goumare, L. (1999), *Contemporary Art Practices: Art as Experience*. Paris: Editions Dis Voir.

Artifice Inc. (2007), 'Great buildings online' [Online] Available: http://www.greatbuildings.com. Accessed August 15 2008.

Atkins, M. (1994), 'Theories of learning and multimedia applications: an overview', *Research Papers in Education*, 8: 2, pp. 251–71.

Baehr, H. and Dyer, G. (eds) (1987), *Boxed In: Women and Television*. London: Pandora.

Baker, K. (2007), 'The problem with unpaid work', *University of St Thomas Law Journal*, Social Science Research Network [Online] Available: http://ssrn.com/abstract=996161. Accessed June 28 2007.

Barthes, R. (1985), *The Fashion System*. London: Cape.

BBC (2005), *Designing for Interactive Television v1.0: BBCi and Interactive TV Programmes*. London: British Broadcasting Corporation.

Beaird, J. (2007), *The Principles of Beautiful Web Design* [Online] Available: http://www.sitepoint.com/print/principles-beautiful-web-design. Accessed August 6 2008.

BECTA (British Educational Communications and Technology Agency) (2005), *Personalised Learning and ICT* [Online] Available: http://foi.becta.org.uk/display.cfm?cfid=662527&cftoken=63d05f972705-4B7DF789-C05D-EAE1-98481165EA7BBC6B&resID=14738. Accessed August 6 2008.

Berenson, M. (2005), *The Business of Fashion, Beauty and Style*. Boston: Aspatore.

Besio, S. and Salminen, A. (2004), 'Children and youngsters and technology', *Technology and Disability*, 16, pp. 115–17.

Boorstin, J. (1990), *The Hollywood Eye: What Makes Movies Work*. Los Angeles: Silman-James Press.

Boud, D.and Miller, N. (eds) (1996), *Working with Experience*. London: Routledge.

Bourriaud, N. (2002), *Relational Aesthetics*. France: Les presses du reel.

Bull, M. (2000), *Sounding Out the City: Personal Stereos and the Management of Everyday Life*. New York: Berg.

Bunning, K. and Heath, R. (forthcoming), 'The advocacy process in young people with intellectual disability: A place for ICT and rich and multiple media?', *Journal of Applied Research in Intellectual Disabilities*.

Burke, Y. (2005), 'Teaching new perspectives: digital space and Flash interactivity', *Digital Creativity*, 16 (3).

Bush-Brown, H. (1976), *Beaux Arts to Bauhaus and Beyond*. New York: Whitney Library of Design.

Bywater, B. (2005), 'Accessibility design guidelines can be simple', *UsabilityNews.com* [Online] Available: http://www.usabilitynews.com/news/article2485.asp. Accessed August 6 2008.

Caine, B., Gatens, M., Grahame, E., Larbalestier, J., Watson, S. and Webby, E. (1998), *Australian Feminism: A Companion*. Melbourne. Oxford University Press.

Campbell, K. (1999), 'The web: Design for active learning', *Academic Technologies for Learning* [Online] Available: http://www.atl.ualberta.ca/documents/articles/activeLearning001.htm. Accessed August 6 2008.

Change Picture Bank [Online] Available: http://www.changepeople.co.uk. Accessed August 6 2008.

Chion, M. (1994), *Audio-Vision: Sound on Screen*. New York: Columbia University Press.

Chorianopoulos, K. (2005), 'User interface design and evaluation in interactive TV', *HERMES Newsletter by ELTRUN*, 32, May–June [Online] Available: http://www.eltrun.aueb.gr/eltrun/publications/eltrun-working-paper-series/issue-no-32-may-june-2005/file. Accessed August 6 2008.

Clarke, A. (2006), *Transcending CSS: the Fine Art of Web Design*, Berkeley: New Riders.

Colquhoun, A. (2002), *Modern Architecture*. Oxford: Oxford University Press.

Cooper, A. (2003), 'The origins of personas' [Online] Available: http://www.cooper.com/journal/2003/08/the_origin_of_personas.html. Accessed August 6 2008.

Cranny-Francis, A. (2005), 'Chapter 4 – Sound', in *Multimedia*. London: Sage Publications.

Cubitt, S. (1998), *Digital Aesthetics*. London: Sage.

Curran, S. (2003), *Convergence Design: Creating the User Experience for Interactive Television, Wireless and Broadband*. Gloucester: Rockport.

Dalgarno, B. (2001), 'Interpretations of constructivism and consequences for Computer Assisted Learning', *British Journal of Educational Technology*, 32: 2, pp. 183–94.

Danielewski, M. (2000), *House of Leaves*. Bath: Doubleday.

Deleuze, G. and Guattari, F. (1987), *A Thousand Plateaus: Capitalism and Schizophrenia*. London: Continuum Press.

Dernie, D. (2006), *Exhibition Design*. New York: W.W. Norton & Co.

Dimond, J. (2007), *Aesthetics and Usability: What Can Interface Design Learn from Painting?* [Online] Available: http://www.blinkinteractive.com/ourexperience/essays/2007/01/aesthetics_andusability_what.php. Accessed January 15 2007.

Dogme95 (1995), 'The vow chastity' [Online] Available: http://www.dogme95.dk. Accessed August 6 2008.

Dovey, J. (ed.) (1996), *Fractal Dreams: New Media in Social Context*. London: Lawrence and Wishart.

Dyer, G. (1987), 'Women and television: An overview', in H. Baehr and G. Dyer (eds), *Boxed In: Women and Television*. London: Pandora.

Emerson, E., Hatton, C., Felce, D. and Murphy, G. (2001), *Learning Disabilities – the Fundamental Facts*. London: The Foundation for People with Learning Disabilities.

England, E. and Finney, A. (1999), *Managing Multimedia: Project Management for Interactive Media*. Harlow: Addison-Wesley.

Eronen, L. (2002), 'Design of interactive television programmes', *CHINZ 2002 Proceedings of the 3rd Annual ACM SIGCHI-NZ Symposium on Computer-Human Interaction*. Hamilton, New Zealand. 11–12 July, pp. 73–78.

Evans, C. and Fan, P. (2002), 'Lifelong learning through the virtual university', *Campus-Wide Information Systems*, 19: 4, pp. 127–34.

Fonix Speech *VoiceIn* [Online] Available: http://www.fonixspeech.com/index.php. Accessed August 6 2008.

Ford, S. (2005), 'Creating quality personas: Understanding the levers that drive user behaviour' [Online] Available: http://www.avenuea-razorfish.com/articles/010305_Quality_Personas.pdf. HTML version accessed August 6 2008.

Forlizzi, J. and Battarbee, K. (2004), 'Understanding Experience in Interactive Systems', *Proceedings of DIS 2004 Conference on Designing Interactive Systems: Processes, Practices, Methods and Techniques*. Cambridge, MA: Association for Computing Machinery.

Garrett, J. (2003), *The Elements of User Experience, User Centered Design for the Web*. New York: New Riders.

Gaver, W. (1986), 'Auditory icons: Using sound in computer interfaces', *Human-Computer Interaction: Journal of Theoretical, Empirical, and Methodological Issues of User Science and of System Design*, 2: 2, pp. 167–77.

Gawlinski, M. (2003), *Interactive Television Production*. Oxford: Focal Press.

Gebhart, L. (2005), 'Fashion changes affect the way we think about ourselves and society', *Copley News Service* [Online] No longer available: http://www.copleynews.com. Accessed June 26 2007.

Geddes, R. (2006), 'Second thoughts: Reflections on winning second prize', in A. Watson (ed.), *Building a Masterpiece: The Sydney Opera House*. Sydney: Powerhouse Publishing.

Glaessner, V. (1990), 'Gendered fictions', in A. Goodwin and G. Whannel (eds), *Understanding Television*. London: Routledge.

Gray, R. and McGregor, F. (2005), 'Labels take strain as fashion is super-sized', *Scotland on Sunday* [Online] No longer available: http://scotlandonsunday.scotsman.com. Accessed March 20 2007.

Greenspan, R. (2003), 'Internet not for everyone' [Online] Available: http://www.clickz.com/stats/big_picture/demographics/article.php/2192251. Accessed April 16 2008.

Grodal, T. (1997), *Moving Pictures: a New Theory of Film Genres, Feelings, and Cognition*. New York: Oxford University Press.

Grove, N., Bunning, K., Porter, J. and Olsson, C. (1999), 'See what I mean: interpreting the meaning of communication by people with severe and profound intellectual disabilities', *Journal of Applied Research in Intellectual Disabilities*, 12, pp. 190–203.

Halleck, D. (1991), 'Watch out Dick Tracy! Popular video in the wake of *Exxon Valdez*', in C. Penley and A. Ross (eds), *Technoculture*. Minneapolis: University of Minnesota Press.

Harrysson, B., Svensk, A. and Johansson, G. (2004) 'How people with developmental disabilities navigate the internet', *British Journal of Special Education*, 31: 3, pp. 138–42.

Harvey, D. (1989), *The Condition of Postmodernity: An Enquiry into the Origins of Cultural Change*. Oxford: Blackwell.

Hawkridge, D. and Vincent, T. (1992), *Learning Difficulties and Computers: Access to the Curriculum*. London: Jessica Kingsley.

Heller, D. (2005), 'Aesthetics and interaction design: Some preliminary thoughts', *Interactions*, September–October [Online] Available: http://portal.acm.org/citation.cfm?doid=1082369.1082400. Accessed August 6 2008.

Holman, T. (1997), *Sound for Film and Television*. Boston: Focal Press.

Howes, D. (2005), 'Architecture of the senses', *Sense of the City Exhibition Catalogue*. Montreal: Canadian Centre for Architecture [Online] Available: http://www.david-howes.com/DH-research-sampler-arch-senses.htm. Accessed August 6 2008.

HREOC (2000), 'Bruce Lindsay Maguire v. Sydney Organizing Committee for the Olympic Games', *Human Rights and Equal Opportunity Commission: Disability Rights* [Online] Available: http://www.hreoc.gov.au/disability_rights/decisions/comdec/2000/DD000120.htm. Accessed August 6 2008.

HumanITy [Online] Available: http://www.humanity.org.uk. Accessed August 6 2008.

Humm, M. (1989), *The Dictionary of Feminist Theory*. New York: Prentice Hall.

Hurst, M. (2007), 'Richard Serra and experience design', *goodexperience.com* [Online] Available: http://www.goodexperience.com/blog/archives/005664.php. Accessed June 28 2007.

Hyman, P. (2004) '"Casual" video games are serious business', *The Hollywood Reporter*, [Online] Available: http://www.hollywoodreporter.com/hr/search/article_display.jsp?vnu_content_id=1000535245. Accessed August 6 2008.

Inclusive New Media Design [Online] Available: http://www.inclusivenewmedia.org. Accessed August 6 2008.

Jackson, S. (1993), *Women's Studies: Essential Readings*. New York: NYU Press.

Jensen, J. (2005), 'Interactive television: New genres, new format, new content', *Proceedings of IE2005: 2nd Australasian conference on interactive entertainment*, ACM International Conference Proceeding Series, vol. 123 [Online] Available: http://portal.acm.org/citation.cfm?id=1109194. Accessed August 6 2008.

Johnson, R. and Hegarty, J. (2003), 'Websites as educational motivators for adults with learning disability', *British Journal of Educational Technology*, 34: 4, pp. 479–86.

Jones, M. (2007), *Skintight: An Anatomy of Cosmetic Surgery*. Oxford: Berg.

Kaji-O'Grady, S. (2006), 'Future fast', *U: magazine*, Sydney: University of Technology Sydney. April.

Kaplan, E. (1983), *Women and Film*. London: Methuen.

Kawamura, Y. (2004), *Fashion-ology: An Introduction to Fashion Studies*. Oxford: Berg.

Kendall, L. (1999), 'Recontextualising "cyberspace": Methodological considerations for online research', in S. Jones (ed.), *Doing Internet Research*. London: Sage.

Kennedy, H. (2008), 'New media's potential for personalisation', *Information, Communication and Society*, 11: 3 (April), pp. 307–25.

Kohler, C. (2007), 'A brief history of architectural styles and movements', *Associated Content* [Online] Available: http://www.associatedcontent.com/article/230545/a_brief_history_of_architectural_styles.html. Accessed 8 May 2007.

Kozel, K. (1998), 'Rethinking the end-user's experience: What filmmakers, teachers and advertisers can teach us', *Emedia Professional*. February.

Kreitzman, L. (1999), *24-hour Society*. London: Profile Books.

Krug, S. (2000), *Don't Make Me Think!* Indianapolis: New Riders.

Larcher, J. (2000), 'Information technology for children with language difficulties', in W. Rinaldi (ed.), *Language Difficulties in an Educational Context*. London: Whurr Publishers, pp. 131–47.

Lawson, H. (2001), *Closure: a Story of Everything*. London: Routledge.

LeDoux, J. (1998), *The Emotional Brain: the Mysterious Underpinnings of Emotional Life*. New York: Touchstone.

Leung, L. (2005), *Virtual Ethnicity: Race, Resistance and the World Wide Web*. Aldershot: Ashgate.

Li, H., Daugherty, T. and Biocca, F. (2003), 'The role of virtual experience in consumer learning', *Journal of Consumer Psychology*, 13: 4, pp. 395–407.

Lowgren, J. (2006), 'Pliability as an experiential quality: Exploring the aesthetics of interaction design', *Artifact*, 1: 2, pp. 85–95, [Online] Available: http://webzone.k3.mah.se/k3jolo/Material/pliabilityFinalPre.pdf. Accessed August 6 2008.

Lu, K. (2005) 'Interaction design principles for interactive television', Master of Science in Information Design and Technology thesis, Georgia Institute of Technology [Online] Available: http://idt.gatech.edu/ms_projects/klu/lu_karyn_y_200505_mast.pdf. Accessed August 6 2008.

Macaulay, C., Benyon, D. and Crerar, A. (2000), 'Voices in the forest: Sounds, soundscapes and interface design', *Towards a Framework for Design and Evaluation of Navigation in Electronic Spaces*, [Online] Available: http://www.sics.se/humle/projects/persona/web/littsurvey/ch10.pdf. Accessed August 6 2008.

McClurg-Genevese, J. (2005a), 'The elements of design', *Digital Web Magazine* [Online] Available: http://www.digital-web.com/articles/elements_of_design. Accessed August 15 2005.

McClurg-Genevese, J. (2005b), 'The principles of design', *Digital Web Magazine* [Online] Available: http://www.digital-web.com/articles/principles_of_design. Accessed August 15 2005.

McGovern, G. (2002), 'The myth of interactivity on the Internet', *New Thinking* [Online] Available: http://gerrymcgovern.com/nt/2002/nt_2002_03_18_interactivity.htm. Accessed August 6 2008.

McKee, R. (1997), *Story: Substance, structure, style, and the principles of screenwriting*. Chatham: Methuen.

McRobbie, A. (1998), *British Fashion Design: Rag or Image Industry?* New York: Routledge.

Mann, P. (1989), 'Portrayal of women in advertising: Self-regulation and other options', *Media Information Australia*, 51 (February).

Meadows, M. (2003), *Pause and Effect: the Art of Interactive Narrative*. Indianapolis: New Riders.

Metros, S. and Hedberg, J. (2002), 'More than just a pretty (inter)face: The role of the graphical user interface in engaging eLearners', *Quarterly Review of Distance Education*, 3: 3, pp. 191–205.

Mulvey, L. (1989), *Visual and Other Pleasures*. London: Macmillan.

Mumby, D. and Putnam, L. (1992), 'The politics of emotion: A feminist reading of bounded rationality', *Academy of Management Review*, 17, pp. 465–86.

Mumford, E. and Henshall, D. (1983), *Designing Participatively: a Participative Approach to Computer Systems Design*. Manchester: Manchester Business School.

Murray, J. (1997), *Hamlet on the Holodeck: the Future of Narrative in Cyberspace*. Cambridge: The MIT Press.

Nakamura, L. (2002), *Cybertypes: Race, Ethnicity and Identity on the Internet*. New York: Routledge.

Nielsen, J. (1999), 'When bad design becomes the standard' [Online] Available: http://www.useit.com/alertbox/991114.html. Accessed August 6 2008.

Nielsen, J. (2000), 'End of web design' [Online] Available: http://www.useit.com/alertbox/20000723.html. Accessed August 6 2008.

Nielsen, J. (2001), 'First rule of usability? Don't listen to users' [Online] Available: http://www.useit.com/alertbox/20010805.html. Accessed August 6 2008.

Nielsen, J. (2005), 'Ten usability heuristics' [Online] Available: http://www.useit.com/papers/heuristic/heuristic_list.html. Accessed August 6 2008.

Nightingale, V. (1990), 'Women as audiences', in M. Brown (ed.), *Television and Women's Culture*. Sydney: Currency.

Norman, D. (1993), *Things That Make us Smart: Defending Human Attributes in the Age of the Machine*. Reading: Addison-Wesley.

Norman, D. (2004), *Emotional Design: Why we Love (or Hate) Everyday Things*. New York: Basic Books.

O'Hara, K. and Stevens, D. (2006), *Inequality.com: Power, Poverty and the Digital Divide*. Oxford: Oneworld.

Parkins, W. and Craig, G. (2006), *Slow Living*. Oxford: Berg.

Pawley, M. (1990), *Theory and Design in the Second Machine Age*. Oxford: Basil Blackwell.

Porter, J. (2006), 'Ugliness, social design, and the MySpace lesson' [Online] Available: http://bokardo. com/archives/do-myspace-users-have-bad-taste. Accessed August 18 2006.

Propp, V. (1968), *Morphology of the Folktale*. Austin: University of Texas Press.

Radway, J. (1984), *Reading the Romance: Woman, Patriarchy and Popular Literature*. Chapel Hill: University of North Caroline Press.

Ramsden, P. (1992), *Learning to Teach in Higher Education*. New York: Routledge, pp. 17–26.

Renblad, K. (2000), 'Persons with intellectual disability and their opportunities to exert influence in their activities and social contacts: An interview study', *Technology and Disability*, 13, pp. 55–65.

Risebero, B. (1992), *Fantastic Form: Architecture and Planning Today*. London: The Herbert Press.

Roy Morgan Research Pty Ltd (January to December 2006) 'Interest in watching sports on payTV'. Melbourne: Roy Morgan Single Source Australia.

Schank, R. and Cleary, C. (1995), *Engines for Education*. Hillsdale: Lawrence Erlbaum Associates.

Sekular, R., Sekular, A. and Lau, R. (1997) 'Sound alters visual motion perception, *Nature*, 385, p. 308.

Shedroff, N. (2001), *Experience Design 1*. Indianapolis: New Riders.

Silverstone, R. (1990), 'Television and everyday life: Towards an anthropology of the television audience', in M. Ferguson (ed.), *Public Communication: the New Imperatives*. London: Sage, pp.173–89.

Skatssoon, J. (2006), 'Web users are quick to judge' [Online] Available: http://www.abc.net.au/news/ newsitems/200601/s1548520.htm. Accessed January 16 2006.

Smith, G. (1999), 'Local Emotions, Global Moods', in C. Plantinga and G. Smith (eds.), *Passionate Views: Film, Cognition and Emotion*. Baltimore: John Hopkins University Press.

Soloway, E. and Pryor, A. (1996), 'The next generation in HCI', *Communications of the ACM*, 39: 4 (April).

Spoerri, D., Filliou, R., Williams, E., Roth, D. and Topor, R. (1962), *An Anecdoted Topography of Chance*. London: Atlas Press.

Stanley, L. (ed.) (1990), *Feminist Praxis: Research, Theory and Epistemology in Feminist Sociology*. London: Routledge.

Storms, R. (1998) 'Auditory-Visual Cross-Modal Perception Phenomena', United States Navy, Naval PostGraduate School doctoral dissertation, [Online] Available: http://gamepipe.usc.edu/~zyda/ Theses/Russell.Storms.PhD.pdf. Accessed July 3 2008.

Tan, E. (1996), *Emotion and the Structure of Narrative Film: Film as an Emotion Machine*. Mahwah: Erlbaum.

Tunstall, J. (1993), *Television Producers*. London: Routledge.

Turkle, S. (1996), *Life on the Screen: Identity in the Age of the Internet*. London: Weidenfeld and Nicholson.

Veblen, T. (1967), *The Theory of the Leisure Class*. London: Penguin.

Vogt, C., Kumrow, D. and Kazlauskas, E. (2001), 'The design elements in developing effective learning and instructional web sites', *Academic Exchange Quarterly*, 5: 4 (Winter), pp. 40–48.

Vroomen, J. and de Gelder, B. (2000), 'Sound enhances visual perception: cross-modal effects of auditory organization on vision', *Journal of Experimental Psychology: Human Perception and Performance*, 26: 5, pp. 1583–1590.

Vroomen, J. and de Gelder, B. (2004), 'Temporal Ventriloquism: Sound Modulates the Flash-Lag Effect', *Journal of Experimental Psychology: Human Perception and Performance*, 30: 3, pp. 513–518.

Walker, D. (2000), 'Personalisation goes one-on-one with reality', *Shorewalker.com* [Online] Available: http://www.shorewalker.com/section1/personalisation_worth.html. Accessed August 6 2008.

Watson, A. (ed.) (2006), *Building a Masterpiece: The Sydney Opera House*. Sydney: Powerhouse Publishing.

Widgit Software [Online] Available: http://www.widgit.com. Accessed August 6 2008.

Williamson, J. (1978), *Decoding Advertisments: Ideology and Meaning in Advertising*. London: Marion Boyars.

World Health Organization (1980), International Classification of Functioning, Disability and Health. Geneva: WHO.

World Health Organization (2001), International Classification of Functioning, Disability and Health (ICF) [Online] Available: http://www.who.int/classifications/icf/en/. Accessed August 6 2008.

World Wide Web Consortium (2004), 'Web Accessibility Initiative' [Online] Available: http://www.w3.org/WAI. Accessed August 6 2008.

World Wide Web Consortium (2004) 'Web Content Accessibility Guidelines' [Online] Available: http://www.w3.org/TR/WCAG20. Accessed August 6 2008.

Wurman, R. (1989), *Information Anxiety*. New York: Doubleday.

Zelanski, P. and Fisher, M. (1988), *The Art of Seeing*. Englewood Cliffs: Prentice-Hall.

LIST OF CONTRIBUTORS

Scott Bryant is an experience architect at News Digital. Prior to studying and working in the information sciences, he studied fine art.

Carla Drago has worked extensively on traditional film, television, documentary and commercials. She has been an executive producer in interactive television for Austar Entertainment and for the digital media agency, Massive Interactive.

Sara Goldstein is a usability expert and experience designer with a strong interest in fashion. She holds a Masters in Interactive Multimedia and has over seven years' experience in website and intranet consulting, design and development. Her clients included Deloitte, Intel and some government agencies; prior to this, she worked for Sapient. She now runs thebargainqueen.org and tastycherry.net.

Dr Helen Kennedy does and teaches interactive media theory and practice, mostly in the Institute of Communications Studies at the University of Leeds. Her research interests span the broad area of new media theory, practice and debate. She is currently researching new media development and cognitive disability. Her interactive media practice includes a range of collaborative projects, on which she has worked as project manager, website builder and CD programmer.

Dr Linda Leung is a senior lecturer at the Institute for Interactive Media and Learning, University of Technology Sydney. She is also a chief investigator on projects for the Australasian Cooperative Research Centre for Interaction Design. She has previously worked at the universities of London, East London, North London, Miami and Western Sydney. Returning to Sydney from London in 1999 to catch the tail-end of the dot.com boom, she consulted in industry in executive producer and project manager roles with clients including government departments, telecommunications companies, non-profit organizations and artists.

Daisy Tam is a PhD student at the Centre for Cultural Studies, Goldsmiths College, University of London. Her dissertation is on the social experience of time and space in relation to food.

Adrienne Tan co-founded Brainmates, a product management agency which has specialized in the development of applications for interactive television. She has an economics background majoring in industrial relations.

Mark Ward is founding director of sound post-production company, Counterpoint Sound, and has designed sound for commercials, documentaries, experimental and low-budget feature films. He teaches at the Australian Film, Television & Radio School (AFTRS) and is writing a PhD entitled 'The Art of Noise: Principles of Sound Design in the Communication of Emotion and Cinematic Narrative'.

Meaghan Waters is a trained architect who has traversed the design of buildings, clothes and online environments. In the process, she has worked as a senior experience modeler at Sapient, before establishing her own consultancy.

INDEX